About Island Press

Island Press, a nonprofit organization, publishes, markets, and distributes the most advanced thinking on the conservation of our natural resources—books about soil, land, water, forests, wildlife, and hazardous and toxic wastes. These books are practical tools used by public officials, business and industry leaders, natural resource managers, and concerned citizens working to solve both local and global resource problems.

Founded in 1978, Island Press reorganized in 1984 to meet the increasing demand for substantive books on all resource-related issues. Island Press publishes and distributes under its own imprint and offers these services to other nonprofit organizations.

Support for Island Press is provided by Apple Computer, Inc., Geraldine R. Dodge Foundation, The Energy Foundation, The Charles Engelhard Foundation, The Ford Foundation, Glen Eagles Foundation, The George Gund Foundation, William and Flora Hewlett Foundation, The Joyce Foundation, The John D. and Catherine T. MacArthur Foundation, The Andrew W. Mellon Foundation, The Joyce Mertz-Gilmore Foundation, The New-Land Foundation, The J. N. Pew, Jr. Charitable Trust, Alida Rockefeller, The Rockefeller Brothers Fund, The Rockefeller Foundation, The Florence and John Schumann Foundation, The Tides Foundation, and individual donors.

About The Conservation Fund

The Conservation Fund creates partnerships to protect land and water resources. Founded in 1985 as a nonmembership, nonprofit organization committed to entrepreneurial spirit and innovation, the fund targets specific priorities with a series of focused natural resource conservation programs.

American Greenways helps communities and states establish public and private open space corridors. The *American Land Conservation Program* of the Richard King Mellon Foundation, assisted by the fund, protects open space, wetlands, and wildlife areas of national significance. The *Civil War Battlefield Campaign* works to safeguard the nation's "hallowed ground" through the acquisition of threatened battlefields and increased community awareness. *Public Conservation Partnerships* assist agencies by buying property, when it is on the market, for public open space. The land is sold to the agency when public funds are available. The *Freshwater Institute* develops economically feasible, scientifically valid, new approaches for the conservation of freshwater resources.

Related programs support the conservation community through improved communication, increased resources, and greater public recognition. The newsletters *Land Letter* and *Common Ground* report on legislation, news, and trends in natural resources and land conservation. The *Alexander Calder Conservation Award,* established by the Union Camp Corporation, annually recognizes cooperation between business and conservation.

Donations from individuals, foundations, and corporations underwrite activities of The Conservation Fund, a 501(c)(3) organization. All contributions are tax deductible to the limit permitted by law.

VOICES from the Environmental Movement

VOICES from the Environmental Movement

PERSPECTIVES FOR A NEW ERA

Edited by Donald Snow

THE CONSERVATION FUND

Foreword by Patrick F. Noonan

ISLAND PRESS

Washington, D.C. ■ *Covelo, California*

Library of Congress Cataloging-in-Publication Data
Voices from the environmental movement : perspectives for a new era /
edited by Donald Snow.
      p.   cm.
   Includes bibliographical references and index.
   ISBN 1-55963-133-3 (acid-free paper).—ISBN 1-55963-132-5 (pbk.
acid-free paper)
   1. Conservation of natural resources—United States.
2. Conservation leadership—United States. 3. Conservationists—
United States. 4. Environmentalists—United States. 5. Green movement—United States.   I. Snow, Donald.
S930.V65   1991
333.7′2′0973—dc20   91-39067
                                                          CIP

Printed on recycled, acid-free paper

Manufactured in the United States of America
10 9 8 7 6 5 4 3 2 1

Contents

Foreword

THE REAL STRENGTH of the conservation and environmental community in the United States is its diversity. Groups from the Peconic Land Trust on Long Island to the Western Washington Toxics Coalition on the Pacific Coast deal with a broad range of issues with an even broader range of practical solutions.

Each organization has its own unique mission, its own resources, its own constituency, and, in a real sense, its own agenda. For many years, a guiding principle behind conservation and environmental activities was summed up in a simple phrase: Think globally, act locally. While that advice is valid today, it does not go far enough. We must add a third element: Work together. Collaboration is vital if we are effectively to manage our limited resources. Today, environmental concerns are too important to be left to environmentalists alone. We must actively engage all sectors of our society.

Collaboration means building partnerships. The experienced leaders who contributed to *Voices from the Environmental Movement* tell us from different perspectives that if we are to achieve the results that are essential for a sustainable Earth, we must marshal our resources—people, knowledge, time, money—toward common goals. The resources that are needed will not come from a single entity. We need the skills and experience from within and without the nonprofit world to address the many complex issues that face it. We need the best and the brightest to help us recycle our own thinking toward a common agenda and to provide knowledgeable and capable leadership.

G. Jon Roush, in his excellent introduction to the articles that follow, suggests that an actual environmental movement does not yet exist in the United States. As a member of the recent President's Commission on Americans Outdoors, I had the privilege to travel throughout the United States and to listen and learn from thousands of Americans about how strongly they support environmental initiatives. While the concerns are felt deeply, they often lack the unity and defined perspective that mark the boundaries of an issue-oriented movement. Unfortunately, conservation lacks the tradition of common "watering holes." There are no forums where volunteers and professionals can share ideas, where land conservation specialists can meet solid waste campaigners, where air quality can meet water quality. There is no place where politicians can find a constituency, no marketplace for funders, and, most importantly, no platform for a continuing dialogue between economic and environmental interests.

The "watering hole" concept—whether the analogy relates to the Serengeti or midtown Manhattan—suggests a coming together to exchange information, to discuss alternatives and, ultimately, to achieve a consensus. The process requires understanding, patience, and a respect for divergent views. It demands looking at the many people and diverse organizations involved in conservation and environmental issues as colleagues, not as adversaries. It calls for an emphasis on networking—matching skills, knowledge, and resources with the tasks that need to be done. We need to broaden the narrow definitions used for conservation and environmental groups to include organizations and people whose specific concerns do not necessarily mirror those of either naturalist John Muir or forester Gifford Pinchot. It is time to move beyond conventional boundaries and to build bridges as we seek to find common ground.

A number of the chapters that follow were written by distinguished members of the advisory committee created to guide the Leadership Project undertaken by The Conservation Fund. Information gathered during the year-long project—masterfully interpreted by editor and project director Donald Snow—was published by Island Press as *Inside the Environmental Movement: Meeting the Leadership Challenge*. That book focuses on current concerns and recommends future actions. *Voices from the Environmental Movement: Perspec-*

tives for a New Era, the companion book, addresses leadership needs and human resources.

Voices from the Environmental Movement is a landmark publication. It takes a first step toward creating "watering holes," toward establishing a common agenda. In *Voices,* leaders with a cross section of environmental backgrounds share their ideas, experiences, and visions. Collectively, their contributions represent the design for a thoughtful, enlightened approach to environmental leadership. Together, the authors show us a path toward a new conservation and environmental ethic that is inclusive rather than exclusive. It is up to us to take the next step, to turn their ideas into action, to create a conservation and environmental movement based on partnerships and focused on accomplishment.

By necessity, conservation and environmental organizations are often forced to concentrate too many resources toward achieving short-term financial goals. In doing so, they sometimes forget that their most important resource is not economic: Their greatest asset is human capital. This book, its companion volume, and the Fund's Conservation Leadership Project are focused on increasing the return on that investment. The dividend is not dollars. The return is measured in a better use of human capital. Better leadership and management skills will create the consensus and enlarge the constituency for a stronger and better nation.

Stimulating market forces to accomplish both environmental goals and those of sustainable economic growth must be our objective. Achieving them will not be simple. Striking the balance between economic progress and environmental protection will take the best managers and leaders America can produce.

It has been a special privilege to serve in the nonprofit environmental field for the past twenty-five years and to share the passion of environmentalism with dedicated volunteers and professionals from across America. These people daily reach beyond personal self-interest to embrace a vision for the United States that reflects long-range goals of conservation and an improved quality of life for everyone. The chapters that follow reflect the experience and wisdom of today's leadership. If we heed their thoughtful teachings, we can design the "watering holes" that will help tomorrow's leaders explore paths of collaboration rather than confrontation. Our future can be brighter than ever before as we help our nation enter a new era that will benefit America and all Americans for generations to come.

Patrick F. Noonan,
President, The Conservation Fund

Acknowledgments

WE WISH TO express our sincerest gratitude to the distinguished members of our advisory council who volunteered their valuable time and expertise: Lamar Alexander, Wallace Dayton, Thomas Deans, George F. Dutrow, George T. Frampton, Jr., Jerry F. Franklin, Ralph E. Grossi, David F. Hales, Jean W. Hocker, Charles R. Jordan, Jack Lorenz, Gerald P. McCarthy, Lyle M. Nelson, Donal C. O'Brien, John C. Oliver, III, James Posewitz, Nathaniel P. Reed, Henry R. Richmond, Daniel Simberloff, Hubert W. Vogelmann, and Norman K. Wessells. We are especially grateful to the outstanding leaders and members of the council who prepared essays for this volume.

We offer special appreciation to those who made the Leadership Project possible, and whose foresight and generosity continue to support the work of conservation and environmental protection organizations. The Compton Foundation, The Ford Foundation, Hanes Family Fund, The William and Flora Hewlett Foundation, George Frederick Jewett Foundation, Morgan Guaranty Trust Company of New York Charitable Trust, Curtis and Edith Munson Foundation, The Pew Charitable Trusts, and the Town Creek Foundation all generously supported this project. The Ford Foundation grant was especially critical to the success of the Minorities Roundtable, whose work is reflected in this volume. Grants from the Munson Foundation and The Pew Charitable Trusts made it possible to publish the results of the study as two volumes.

Two individuals deserve special recognition. Laurie L. Hall took time from her pursuit of a forestry degree at the University of Montana to give tireless service to the Leadership Project. Her good cheer and deft organization contributed enormously to the effort's success.

Kent Curtis, office manager of Canyon Consulting, worked on the numerous changes in the final manuscripts and managed the blizzards of paper.

Finally, we offer our thanks to Barbara Dean and Barbara Youngblood, our editors at Island Press; to the staff of The Conservation Fund, especially for the enthusiastic support of Kiku Hoagland Hanes; and to Jack Lynn, who served as executive editor for The Conservation Fund. Their persistence and patience led to the publication of two separate volumes from the Leadership Project. Their judicious and professional work has made this an infinitely more readable and useful book. They are committed conservationists who labor fully in the spirit of this project.

Patrick F. Noonan,
President, The Conservation Fund

G. Jon Roush,
Senior Associate to the Project

Donald Snow,
Project Director and Editor

VOICES from the
Environmental
Movement

Introduction

G. JON ROUSH
President, Canyon Consulting, Inc.

AFTER THEY HAD introduced themselves and he had shown her around the garden, Adam might have said, "Eve, we live in an age of transition." It has always been so, but in some periods, change seems to accelerate. For the environmental movement, this is one of those periods.

In the past few years, environmental issues have moved near the top of most Americans' list of concerns. Every state now has sizable bureaucracies of environmental regulators. Whole nations are developing environmental strategies, with billions of dollars of commerce at stake. Multinational corporations, with revenues larger than many nations', have phalanxes of lawyers, engineers, and environmental officers, all devoted to keeping the company out of trouble. Even the problems seem larger: global warming, mass extinctions, acid rain.

Such developments are radically changing the conditions within which the environmental movement works. As the essays in this book prove, equally important changes are at work within the movement. It is expanding, diversifying, and reexamining some venerable assumptions. A small social and political movement is changing into something else. What that something else will be is unclear, but it will not appear in a vacuum. The outcome will be influenced by a tangle of forces—values, traditions, and taboos; politics, economics, technology, and science; institutions, corporations, and governments. Nongovernmental environmental organizations cannot control that tangle of forces, but with forethought and will, they can influence it. That tangle of forces is the subject of this book.

This book is one of several outcomes of the Conservation Leadership Project, which was conceived and managed by The Conservation Fund. The Conservation Leadership Project investigated the characteristics, conditions, and needs of environmental leaders in the United States, especially volunteers and professional leaders of nonprofit organizations. Our goal was to produce useful recommendations for enhancing the quality of leadership in the environmental movement. We surveyed and interviewed environmental leaders. We investigated academic programs intended to educate future environmental leaders. We worked closely with a hardworking advisory committee of twenty-one leaders in government, academia, business, and state and national nongovernmental organizations. Our findings and recommendations from that research appear in the companion book *Inside the Environmental Movement*.

That analysis told us a great deal about the inner workings of the environmental movement, but it did not address the tangle of external forces. To describe that context, we commissioned these essays. The authors are uniquely qualified. Each is a leader in his or her own right. Some are centrally involved in the environmental movement, others tangentially. All are thoughtful analysts. We asked each to write about a specific large theme or force that helps shape environmental leaders' own environment. The essays describe the diverse conditions within which decision makers in the environmental movement act. Each essay addresses a key vector constraining and shaping the choices open to environmental leaders.

We did not hope for definitive or exhaustive treatments. The movement is too large, diverse, and mercurial for that. These are personal, speculative, and reportorial essays. Yet underneath the diversity are some common currents that reappear in unexpected ways.

Trying to understand the current state of the conservation movement, we concentrated on leadership for three reasons. First, this is a movement accustomed to extraordinary leadership. The pantheon is awesome: the legendary elders John Muir and Gifford Pinchot; Bob Marshall, the wilderness maker; Aldo Leopold and Rachel Carson, who turned science into ethics; the majestic troublemakers, from Rosalie Edge to David Brower; the policymakers, from Teddy Roosevelt to Stewart and Morris Udall. These and hundreds of others have left their *individual* marks on history. Because of each of them, something changed. Now that the world is awakening to the environmental crisis, change is a certainty, and we naturally look to today's leaders and inquire about their goals and circumstances.

The second reason we have focused on leaders is, paradoxically, that permanent change in the twentieth-century United States has always been effected by groups. Since John Muir and the Sierra Club, every great leader of conservation has counted on an organization of dedicated citizens to institutionalize the vision. All the heroes named in the preceding paragraph were active leaders in major environmental organizations. Now these groups and thousand of others have other leaders. Some are charismatic public figures, while others shun public notice but still lead their groups with skill and passion. Some are not even the titular leaders of their organizations. These leaders will make the decisions that make the groups that make or break the environmental movement. For every public Bob Marshall, there have been hundreds of unrecognized but effective leaders. This book is about their world.

The third reason is that the arena is suddenly much larger. If the nongovernmental environmental movement is to be effective in that world, its leadership will be judged as a whole. We are interested not just in the leadership of individual organizations, but in the strategies and skills that the movement *as a whole* applies to moving the entire cause forward. It will not be enough to build successful organizations; leaders need to plan and form strategic alliances for the common good. These essays examine some social, political, philosophical, and scientific currents with which they must contend.

With change comes turmoil. That is the subtext that underlies these essays. For the movement, this is not only an age of transition; it is an age of conflict, contradiction, and ambiguity. Conflict is a hallmark of the environmental movement's relationships—internal and external. It is sometimes debilitating, especially when groups compete unnecessarily for money or support, but it is also a source of creativity and renewal. In recent years several theorists of organizational development have analyzed the creative use of conflict.[1] Any group needs to contain opposing forces to stay alert and alive. One side or the other might prevail temporarily, but an organization that cannot nurture conflict soon stagnates. (Of course, this is not a new idea; it would not have been novel to Hegel, Blake, Montaigne, Plato, or Confucius.) In his classic study of leadership, James Mac-Gregor Burns goes so far as to argue that successful leaders intentionally build conflict into their organizations, and then nourish that conflict as "a goad to complacent doctrine."[2]

The environmental movement is blessed with plenty of goads to complacent doctrine. In his essay in this book, Nathaniel Reed pinpoints an important one, summarized by a quotation from historian Stephen Fox: The conservation movement is a series of "collisions of professionals and amateurs." As the professional leader of federal agencies and the inspiration for a generation of amateurs, Reed has felt many such collisions, and he knows both sides. His esteem for relentlessly dedicated amateurs as the driving force of environmental change balances his respect for savvy insiders who know how to get things done. The need is not just to have both sides; they must "collide." Forget any utopian hopes of perfect comity; progress often comes through confrontation, and that requires not getting too cozy with the insiders. As Reed says: "Something becomes politically impossible because all of us in the loop—the administration officials, the Hill staffers, the environmental lobbyists—talk to each other and agree that it's out of bounds. Sometimes it takes an outsider, even a flake, to remind us that there is no virtue in failing even to try."

Reed's fear that the crucial energy of amateur generalists may disappear with the "professionalization" of the nonprofit movement is echoed in many of these essays (as it was in the questionnaires and interviews of the Conservation Leadership Project). It is a complex question. The data of the Conservation Leadership Project indicate that over half the thousands of environmental organizations in the United States have no paid staff and rely entirely on volunteers, and it seems reasonable to assume that at least half of the remainder could not survive without their active volunteers. It is true that many environmental organizations, especially the larger ones, have become increasingly professional in their management, but even some of the very largest still find essential work for thousands of volunteers. Still, we have found a prevailing worry as to whether volunteers are being dealt out of the game by large groups' reliance on direct mail and multimillion-dollar fund-raising campaigns, and by the growing complexity of issues requiring high-technology and technical expertise.

As Jack Lorenz points out in his essay, the growth of interest in environmental issues has brought even more volunteers and has challenged the movement to use their abilities and enthusiasm to do real work. His survey of volunteer programs in some of the largest organizations, including his own, shows a respect for volunteer contributions and some creative programs for tapping volunteer strength. Yet something still seems to be missing. "Why," he asks, "if more than three-fourths of the people consider themselves environmentalists and a large percentage rank environmental protection as the country's top concern, are our elected officials not jumping at our command?" Could it be that environmental leaders have not yet expressed what the grass roots really want to say?

Sounding the theme again in her essay, Sally Ranney celebrates the power of "spontaneous, 'unprofessional' leadership." In talking about the power of outsiders, she takes the matter further, highlighting the role of women in countering machismo attitudes toward nature and toward social issues, even within the movement. A telling characteristic of the nonprofit environmental movement is the relative shortage of female leaders in larger national and international organizations. That scarcity contrasts with the predominance of female leaders in local organizations, especially those fighting public health issues like hazardous-waste dump siting. These women are taking on not just the establishment; they are taking on the *male* establishment. They are championing values of nurturing and mutuality that our culture does not often encourage men to prize and develop. It is ironic that women have appeared so infrequently among professional national environmental leaders when remarks about "little old ladies in tennis shoes" and more blatant sexual slurs are still lobbed at the movement.

In that light, the "collision" between amateurs and professionals within the movement is analogous to the collision between the conservation movement and the larger society. It is the collision between distilled passion and the pragmatic values of people at work. Within the movement, the collision is between outsiders and the mavens who are responsible for getting things done. In the larger world, it is "the environment versus jobs." Since the beginning—since Thoreau and earlier—the gentle pastime of loving nature has often led, with sad inevitability, to such collisions.

Why has environmentalism so often been seen as a dangerous, antisocial, even un-American, activity? True, some radical and violent things have been done in the name of the environment, but most people involved in the movement are solid Americans, trying to earn a living and stay true to solid American values. Why are other people predisposed to assume that environmental activists would prefer to live in caves and eat nuts and berries, dragging the entire economy down with them? Some reasons are obvious. Extremists make good press, and so they get more column inches than their more moderate peers. Beyond that, environmental values shine the light on some contradictions in American culture. For example, Americans have valued the frontier both as a place of wild nature and as a place to make fortunes by exploiting that nature. Americans love the land, and they also love to exploit its bounty for their own benefit. We have lived with that contradiction by emphasizing one side or the other as suits the occasion. When environmentalists suggest that the land-loving side is always preferable, they tip the balance uncomfortably and provoke defense mechanisms from denial to name-calling to worse.

One strong segment of the environmental movement follows the logic of this position to a challenging conclusion. It is the unsettling idea that as a species, human beings are no more important than any other species. The classic development of this idea is Aldo Leopold's essay "The Land Ethic": "In short, a land ethic changes the role of *Homo sapiens* from conqueror of the land-community to plain member and citizen of it."[3] This idea posits Nature herself as the ultimate outsider, the not-to-be-denied "goad to complacent doctrine." She insists that she be listened to, with an indifference to the arguments of boardrooms and caucuses that would make other ladies in tennis shoes proud.

The earliest great example of the conflict between the rights of nature and the rights of human beings was the fight over California's Hetch Hetchy Dam at the beginning of the twentieth century. The story is often told in mythic terms as exemplifying the two dominant currents in U.S. natural resource policy. No wonder, for rarely does reality offer such powerful mythic elements. Two charismatic, visionary opponents vie for the mind of a powerful president, Teddy Roosevelt, in a choice between the needs of a great wilderness area (Yosemite) and those of a booming, romantic city (San Francisco).

One opponent, John Muir, was Wilderness personified. Like Thoreau, he was a recluse with an almost inadvertent flair for self-promotion. Unlike Thoreau, he was bigger than life, as Yosemite is bigger than Walden. He took to riding out Sierra thunderstorms in the wind-tossed tops of sequoias or crossing pencil-thin ice bridges across glacial crevasses in Alaska—and then writing hugely popular accounts of his exploits. A ferocious defender of the wilderness, he had already helped found the Sierra Club when he crossed his former ally Gifford Pinchot.

Pinchot was a German-trained forester, a dedicated conservationist, and an accomplished politician. In an era when felling forests was still God's work—and the loggers' hero was Paul Bunyan, who could clear-cut forty acres before breakfast—Pinchot was the voice of the future. "Wise use" was to replace wanton exploitation, and Pinchot's new Forest Service was the agency that would make it happen. Those who make use of nature—for example, farmers, hunters, or foresters—often also love it, and some have accounted for great conservation victories. Still, the battle between *conservation* (the "wise use" of natural resources) and *preservation* ("hands off") was joined over Hetch Hetchy, and persists today.

The conflict between conservation and preservation seemed a clear difference in values, but to Teddy Roosevelt, the resolution was anything but clear. He had personally championed both opponents. He had slept in the snow under the stars with Muir while local developers, his would-be hosts and Muir's enemies, searched Yosemite in vain for him. He had then gone on to sign the bill that finally saved Yosemite and propelled the National Park System into the twentieth century. Roosevelt himself had written: "There are no words that can tell of the hidden spirit of the wilderness, that can reveal its mystery, its melancholy, and its charm."[4]

On the other hand, he had also defended Pinchot against the wilderness lovers. In his first annual message to Congress (1901), Roosevelt had said: "The fundamental idea of forestry is the perpetuation of forests by use. Forest protection is not an end in itself; it is a means to increase and sustain the resources of our country and the industries which depend on them."[5] Soon after that, Roosevelt would need to wheel around to the other flank and protect Pinchot against powerful timber interests, who raised the specter of lost jobs, economic devastation, and unconstitutional government influence. No matter how close they get to the center of power, even the most privileged conservationists, like Gifford Pinchot, can still feel like outsiders.

The Hetch Hetchy Valley was in a primitive area that had been set aside when Yosemite was declared a park. San Francisco needed the water that a dammed Hetch Hetchy could deliver. Listen first to Muir on the subject of Hetch Hetchy, with the rhetoric of prophets (1912): "These temple destroyers, devotees of ravaging commercialism, seem to have a perfect contempt for Nature, and instead of lifting their eyes to the God of the Mountains, life them to the Almighty Dollar." Then Pinchot, with the rhetoric of cost-benefit analysis (1913): "I am fully persuaded that . . . the injury . . . by substituting a lake for the present swampy floor of the valley . . . is altogether unimportant compared to the benefits to be derived from its use as a reservoir."[6]

Both sides launched national public relations campaigns. The issue divided not only the nation but the conservation movement. For example, Warren Olney, a Sierra Club founder, supported the dam. Roosevelt—part preservationist, part conservationist, and politician through and through—temporized and vacillated on the issue until he left office, as did his successor, William Howard Taft. Finally, in 1913, the Senate decided in favor of the reservoir, and the new president, Woodrow Wilson, refused to veto the bill. His language explaining the decision was curiously tepid, in contrast with the national passion that years of debate had generated: "The bill was opposed by so many public-spirited men . . . that I have naturally sought to scrutinize it very closely. I take the liberty of thinking that their fears and objections were not well founded."[7]

The decision itself seems less important than the dramatic conflict and its impact on Americans' conscience. We have endured many other environmental battles, many of them at least as important as Hetch Hetchy ecologically and socially, but it is Hetch Hetchy that we remember. Roosevelt's dilemma, the Muir versus Pinchot dilemma, is familiar to anyone who is serious about conservation. The tension between the two worldviews is part of our culture. Even if we know how we would have voted on Hetch Hetchy, the underlying issue touches something uncomfortably familiar. There must, we think, be a solution. That is why we keep retelling the story.

(The Hetch Hetchy fight presaged other conflicts as well. For example, Sally Ranney quotes the San Francisco city engineer deriding opponents in 1913 as "short-haired women and long-haired men," an early example of the deeper, darker masculine defensiveness that continues to obstruct dialogue today.)

There is no *right* tradition—conservation, environmentalism, preservation, deep ecology, human ecology, or whatever—no single definition that fits all of this diverse and turbulent movement. Nor is it always possible to know who is outside or inside. That is partly a matter of perspective. To many loggers and miners in my part of the country (the Northern Rockies), Muir's descendant Sierra Club is a symbol of everything that is dangerously radical and vaguely socialistic about environmentalists. Yet some truly radical environmentalists see it as an overgrown relic that doesn't go nearly far enough.

The history of the movement can be seen as successive waves of outsiders moving toward the center. As they get closer, new waves begin to form on the horizon, and to them, the old outsiders look like insiders. Today's outsiders include the thousands of small, local organizations described by Charles Jordan and Donald Snow in their essay on ethnic and racial minorities in the environmental movement.

These intensely political groups are creating a movement of their own, a universe parallel with and often invisible to the mainstream environmental groups. Leaders of these grass-roots groups, who reach their constituents face to face, not through direct mail, see *their* groups as the mainstream.

Will these two movements find a way to build on each other's strengths? If history were a guide, we would not ask for assimilation or capitulation. We would settle for a good collision, like two basketball players going after the same ball. For that to happen, you have to acknowledge that you are in the same game. Such collisions spring from at least enough mutual respect and curiosity to recognize a worthy opponent, and they can be a first step toward learning and progress.

Another group of outsiders, in some ways more exotic but less threatening to the larger U.S. groups, are nongovernmental organizations in other countries. A generation of professional conservationists has recognized the importance of transnational conservation. With growing sophistication, they have focused on the tropics, where most of the planet's biodiversity resides and where many of the forces driving the biosphere originate. The World Wildlife Fund had already established a consortium of nationally based groups by 1970, and in the 1970s and 1980s, other U.S. groups developed international programs. After several abortive starts, a few began to establish partnerships with indigenous organizations.

At first, the U.S. groups offered money and technical support, while the indigenous groups offered access, cultural sensitivity, and legitimacy. As foreign organizations have proliferated and grown more sophisticated, and as more U.S. groups enter the field, the relationships have grown more complex. Aldemaro Romero, the leader of Venezuela's BIOMA—a particularly effective and creative group—traces the complexities in his essay. In a short time, conservationists have created the basis for an effective network throughout the Western Hemisphere and beyond. As Romero explains, that network's success will depend on everyone's ability to set aside institutional self-interest and respond to the real needs for conservation. It depends on the highest order of leadership, in a world where everyone is an outsider to someone else.

Where, then, is the core? Warren Bennis and Burt Nanus have suggested that "managers are people who do things right and leaders are people who do the right thing."[8] That's easy to say, but the environmental movement works in a confusing and fluid world, with conflicting constituencies, highly complex and often highly technical issues, and usually grossly inadequate information. In such a world, how is a leader to know what the "right thing" is? Where can environmental leaders turn for advice, training, and certainty? Three essays address this question: Daniel Simberloff's, on science in conservation; James Crowfoot's, on academic training programs; and Joanna Underwood's, on environmental ethics.

Simberloff describes this period in biology as (dare we say it?) an age of transition. He offers a caveat that embattled environmental leaders probably would rather not hear: "Conservation biology is so new that . . . its theories are untested. One must therefore view suggestions for specific courses of action with extreme caution." When leaders receive a message like that, shooting the messenger crosses their minds. They sympathize with Harry Truman looking for a one-armed economist, one who couldn't say, "On the other hand . . ." Yet the tentative voice of science is essential. All successful leaders experience moments when they are 51 percent sure but need to act 100 percent sure. That is proper. The danger comes later, when they forget the platform of uncertainty from which they took their necessary leap. If that happens, they become fanatics.

The collision of science and action may seem like a problem, but from another perspective, it is a strength of the environmental movement. At base the movement has scientific integrity or it has nothing. It also has a pragmatism born from tough politics and scrappy fundraising. Environmental leaders know the headaches of making payroll and the practical advantages of overstating an emergency in order to land the gift that makes the difference. When, late at night, they wonder whether they are doing the right thing, they have only two things to fall back on: an ethical compass and honest science. Simberloff describes the current state of conservation biology with honesty and precision, the two qualities that leaders should demand of any scientific advisor. Leaders should neither accept scientific advice unquestioningly nor forget it. They should collide with it.

Simberloff offers his own clear-eyed assessment of the limits of science: "The problem of wastes in the ocean has been heralded at least since Rachel Carson published *Silent Spring* in 1962, but concern about the marine environment seems to have been crystallized recently more by closed beaches and garbage washing ashore than by years of scientific concern over dwindling populations of various marine species." Both sides—science and action—need each other, and they need leaders who know which aspect to emphasize at the moment.

James Crowfoot argues similarly that academia and activists need each other. Academia needs activists to advocate relevant research and help set research priorities. "At the same time," he says, "the conservation movement could improve its work on environmental problems by recognizing the need for research-based information to guide the implementation of practices that will lessen environmental problems. In the heat of crisis and with the energy and commitment of a movement, it is all too easy to act in ways that are well intentioned but ill informed, and that do not result in the intended effects." The problem again is not that conservation has different modes—this time, activist and academic—but that they do not engage each other enough.

Crowfoot then mounts a daunting challenge to the academic establishment. He is worth quoting at length:

> The challenge in the face of the deepening environmental crisis is for institutions of higher learning to establish explicit policies that acknowledge the crisis and the actions needed to alleviate it while establishing patterns of global sustainability. Failure to do so is tantamount to supporting the status quo and actively contributing to the fundamental crisis. If they pursue this unfortunate course, they will become inhospitable places for environmental and natural resource educators and researchers, and will fail to provide leadership in the face of the threat to the biosphere.

To the extent that colleges and universities continue to promote the myth of value-free scholarship, they will inhibit the evolution of multiple methods of inquiry and synthesis, and fail to provide active debate on the relationship of various scholarly methods to the environmental crisis and what is needed to alleviate it.

"Sustainability," as it is usually conceived, describes a system in which human societies and natural systems exist in an equilibrium that can sustain itself indefinitely. It transcends the preservation-conservation dichotomy. Crowfoot argues that it can begin in a university, with its relative calm, the specialized tools and knowledge of academic specialists, and its opportunities for cross-disciplinary thought and research. "Ultimately," he says, "universities will be asked to help answer the profound question of the twenty-first century: What is the meaning of sustainability and how can it be accomplished?"

Can we *imagine* a sustainable world? Can we describe the politics, economics, science, and culture within which human beings could meet their needs while keeping natural systems intact and functioning? If so, Crowfoot argues, universities will need to recognize that this is an age of transition and change their ways. They will need to change curricula, institute different programs, hire different faculty, use new technologies, establish new collaborative relationships and, of course, spend more money.

Joanna Underwood explores the strengths and shortcomings of science from another direction. Simberloff and Crowfoot are concerned primarily with the theoretical underpinnings of conservation, while Underwood examines the possibilities of technological remediation. She finds some problems:

1. The environmental problems we confront are infinitely more complex than we imagined in 1970.
2. The solutions we sought, largely involving pollution-control technical fixes, have had much less success than hoped for.
3. While we have become more aware of our environmental dilemma, our actions suggest that we have a long way to go in

fully accepting and acting on the meaning of an environmental ethic.

To illustrate the sciences' difficulty in penetrating public perception, Simberloff used the example of marine waste, and Underwood makes the same point with landfills: "While global warming, acid rain, and deforestation are broad issues with long-term implications for life on the planet, the issue of waste has perhaps most directly caused Americans to confront the question of their environmental ethic. Waste brings the issue home to our communities, our streets, our own backyards." Solid scientific data cannot match the impact of something stinking up the neighborhood.

For Underwood, Crowfoot's challenge will not be met without an ethical transformation and a political commitment: "To achieve a sustainable life on this planet will mean curbing our zealous appetites for production and consumption as well as making some major investments in helping developing nations find an economically and socially sustainable means of living."

These essays collectively describe a movement that is in transition in several dimensions. Its world is different from the world of a generation ago. Environmental issues have become part of the national agenda, with an increasingly diverse constituency. New kinds of organizations have appeared, and older groups face new challenges. What has not changed is human nature. The movement is fraught with contradictions and conflict. It includes conflicting ideologies, conflicting strategies, disparate roles and talents, and a climate of organizational competition. In many respects, it also remains a movement of outsiders. Despite the widespread support for environmental values (at least according to the polls), the movement is far from gaining its goals and, by some important measures, is losing ground.

Given that context, what should we ask of environmental leaders? Leadership is something of a hot topic these days, for good reasons, and readers who want to analyze it more deeply than I will here can find several excellent books.[9] Some principles, however, are important. Leaders, James MacGregor Burns argues, should be judged by their ability to create intended, permanent, institutional change.[10] In a world as changeful and uncertain as the world of the environmental movement, that seems like a good place to begin. Certainly the goal of environmental leaders is to create change. They want to develop their organizations into the best ones possible, and to help their organizations continue to change and adapt to new conditions. They also want to create change in the world around them, to implant their values in American institutions and mores. In both their own organizations and the larger world, some kind of change will happen no matter what. The test will be whether the changes are what the leaders intend.

How leaders create change is as important as their results. Obviously, they accomplish their ends through other people, but they have a specific relationship with those people. We do not have an adequate word for a leader's group. I will use the customary word *followers,* although that implies a more passive role than those people play. In fact, leaders make their followers more powerful. That is why the use of coercive power is the opposite of leadership. Leaders empower their followers by giving voice to their aspirations and by giving them the confidence that they can do great things.

Leadership comes in all styles—theatrical, militant, coaching, nurturing, quiet—practically any style except bullying or passive. We should not demand a particular style from environmental leaders, or any others, because leadership requires integrity and credibility. Trying to adopt a "leadership style" that is not true to the leader's personality is a formula for almost certain failure. In our interviews for the Conservation Leadership Project, we found many personalities, but we also found three constants: Effective leaders are thoroughly committed to the cause, they understand their followers, and they understand their political and cultural environment.

The essays in this book reveal another constant. For the foreseeable future, environmental leaders will have to deal well with conflict. There are actually three concentric circles of conflict. The first is conflict within individual organizations. Surrounding that are conflicts

among organizations within the movement. Finally, there are conflicts between the movement and less hospitable parts of the American culture.

Leaders, as I have already noted, always need to accommodate and
perhaps even encourage conflict among their own constituents. As a
manager and a consultant to environmental organizations, I have
found that managing conflict is the most difficult challenge. Most of
the external forces that these essays describe also penetrate into organizations. Besides the normal conflicts of role and personality, every
environmental organization of any size has its internal conservationists and preservationists, grass-roots advocates and technicians, doers
and philosophers, and, increasingly, men and women. The successful
organizations relish those differences and experiment with them.
They are a source of strength. Without effective leadership, however,
they will hamstring the organization.

The next circle—conflicts within the movement—is also difficult.
In the essay that follows, I argue that we do not yet have a truly national environmental movement and we need to create one. That
would require that groups now competing with each other for mea-
ger resources find ways to collaborate, or at least to stay out of each
other's way. Collaboration begins only when the leaders want it. It
requires a mutual decision, when leaders from one group agree with
leaders of another group on compatible goals and strategies.

Environmental leaders should not try to eliminate conflict with
other environmental leaders (assuming such a condition were remotely possible). They must simply work to make the conflict more
systematic, deliberate, and coordinated. The United States and Great
Britain have been allies for well over a century, but they compete
vigorously in many arenas, and the world is better for it. That kind
of conflict is healthy because it stimulates innovation but also recognizes common goals and a common worldview. The conflict among
environmental groups often seems more like that between the United
States and Iraq, except that no one can afford missiles.

Yet the truly difficult conflicts are those between environmental
values and other values in our society. To quote Joanna Underwood
one more time:

Industries under the momentum of production, job creation, and sales don't take lightly to the notion of *not* doing things they have been doing, of *not* producing what they can produce. Likewise, men and women, able to afford a glut of consumer products, haven't taken lightly to the notion of *not* buying and having them. Convenience, near-term gain, and comfort still triumph in day-to-day decisions. The problem now does not seem to be a lack of technologies or scientific information, or of public policy recommendations. . . . The problem seems to be one mainly involving an underlying ethic stimulating much more dramatic change.

Compared with that, the ideological differences among conservation, environmental, and preservation groups are small fry.

The challenge implicit in these essays is the old American challenge: *e pluribus unum.* Can environmentalists, by traveling separate ways, show each other and all Americans possibilities that will bring us together, hold us together, and save the world? Beyond that, can we find or invent the leadership that will make those possibilities real, that will give us, stragglers and all, the vision and courage to do the right thing?

Notes

1. For example, Richard Tanner Pascale, *Managing on the Edge: How the Smartest Companies Use Conflict to Stay Ahead* (New York: Simon and Schuster, 1990); Thomas Crum, *The Magic of Conflict* (New York: Simon and Schuster, 1987); Peter Elbow, *Embracing Contraries* (New York: Oxford University Press, 1987); David A. Lax and James K. Sebenios, *The Manger as Negotiator* (New York: Free Press, 1986).
2. James MacGregor Burns, *Leadership* (New York: Harper and Row, 1979), 453.
3. Aldo Leopold, "The Land Ethic," in *A Sand County Almanac and Sketches Here and There* (New York: Oxford University Press, 1987), 204.
4. "African Game Trails," in *The Winning of the West, The Works of Theodore Roosevelt,* cited by Roderick Nash, *Wilderness and the American Mind,* rev. ed. (New Haven: Yale University, 1973), 150.
5. Quoted by Nash, *Wilderness and the American Mind,* 162.
6. Both Muir and Pinchot quoted by Nash, *Wilderness and the American Mind,* 161.
7. Nash, *Wilderness and the American Mind,* 179–80.

8. Warren Bennis and Burt Nanus, *Leaders: The Strategies for Taking Charge* (New York: Harper and Row, 1985), 21.
9. For example, see Burns, *Leadership;* Bennis and Nanus, *Leaders;* John W. Gardner, *On Leadership* (New York: Free Press, 1990); Edgar H. Schein, *Organizational Culture and Leadership: A Dynamic View* (San Francisco: Jossey Bass, 1990).
10. Burns, *Leadership,* 413ff.

1 Conservation's Hour— Is Leadership Ready?

G. JON ROUSH
President, Canyon Consulting, Inc.

CONSERVATIONISTS ARE ABOUT to lose the war by appearing to win some battles. They are about to receive the wrong kind of help, whether they want it or not. They can change the outcome only by the most difficult of actions—only by changing themselves.

The past twenty-five years have seen some important conservation victories, but they have been mostly local victories. We have cleaned up rivers and lakes, established parks, and set aside natural areas. Even when we have been successful with national issues, we have done so by incrementally protecting specific places. We have augmented national systems of protected areas with millions of acres of beautiful and ecologically important places: wild and scenic rivers, wilderness areas, national parks, and forest land. And we have taken significant steps to improve the management of much of that land.

On the other hand, once we get beyond the protection of specific places and ecosystems, victories are much more difficult to come by. We are losing the fight to protect continental and global systems, and in the long run, those systems will determine the staying power of many of our local successes. Three large global systems in particular are suffering accelerating decline: the air, the oceans, and the biosphere itself.

The Air

In 1970 Congress ordered the Environmental Protection Agency to regulate 320 air pollutants. The EPA went to work immediately. Study spawned study. Scientists and consultants waged profitable war arguing about the number of milligrams that could dance in a ton. In the intervening two decades, although the particulate and sulfur dioxide levels in some major cities have decreased, the total number of U.S. cities violating clean-air standards increased to over 100. In the coy language of the EPA, two of every three U.S. citizens now live in areas of "air-quality non-attainment." According to the Harvard School of Public Health, air pollution contributes to one out of every twenty premature deaths in the United States. According to the American Academy of Pediatrics, air pollutants in most cities could scar children's lungs permanently. Meanwhile, every year the United States alone pours another 2.7 billion tons of pollutants into the air. Of those 320 air pollutants that Congress targeted in 1970, a grand total of 7 had been regulated by mid-1989.

The Oceans

Life was created in the sea and, increasingly, that is where it ends. For years mariners have reported that no part of the seas is free of visible oil slicks. Newsworthy tanker accidents are greeted with newsworthy hearings, but in fact the number of tanker spills and the amount of oil lost have both declined dramatically in the last decade. What is not making the news is the daily insult of sewage sludge, industrial waste, and dredged materials that continue to poison food chains and destroy delicate marine ecosystems. Human beings dump 10 trillion tons of pollutants into the oceans annually. The EPA considers a beach dangerous if nineteen people per thousand are likely to contract a viral infection there in one year. Whether that is the right standard is almost irrelevant. As more beaches close each year, it is the trend that should concern and frighten us.

The Biosphere

Around the world approximately one species becomes extinct every hour, hour after hour, day after day. Experts disagree about the "normal" rate of extinction, but one can conservatively say that today's rate is at least 100 times the average historical rate. The terrifying fact is that extinction continues to accelerate. As one species becomes extinct, others that depend on it also die. As extinction continues, the chances for further extinctions multiply. In many ecosystems we are already on the verge of an extinction avalanche, with hundreds or thousands of species at risk. Once the avalanche begins, some species will disappear quickly, while others may hang on for 200 or 300 years. Whatever the schedule, human intervention may slow the collapse and even rescue some species, but momentum remains on the side of annihilation. Our grandchildren will almost certainly inhabit a planet with half the number of species that inhabit ours. Although the consequences of such biotic impoverishment are incalculable, we can be sure that they will be disastrous. We do know that as the fabric of our biosphere is weakened, so inevitably are the intricate life-support systems on which humankind depends. The Endangered Species Act was designed to dampen such madness. If actually enforced, it could do so. But the laborious process of adding even one species to the list of protected species can take years, thanks largely to the opposition of special interests.

Conservationists say that politics, bureaucratic infighting, and powerful interests—not individual actions—are destroying our environment. They have a good case. For example, the most important cause of extinction is probably habitat loss and habitat alteration. An increasingly worrisome cause of habitat alteration is global warming. And the cause of global warming? Air pollution again. If the greenhouse effect is in fact heating up the earth, then the need to control carbon dioxide output is crucial. Each year we add 3 billion more tons of carbon dioxide to the atmosphere than green-leaved plants can remove. For that reason, we are right to worry about the loss of tropical forests.

Yet U.S. automobiles contribute much more to the CO_2 imbalance than does Brazilian logging. In fact, the United States accounts for almost one-fourth of all CO_2 put into the air from human sources, most of it from burning fossil fuel. Meanwhile, Congress and the White House remain receptive to requests from the automobile industry to extend deadlines for stricter emission standards, even though evidence suggests that those standards could be met with minimal economic pain. And while we wring our hands about the loss of tropical forests, U.S. timber companies are cutting down our own forests at rates above replacement, with the active complicity of the public agencies that are supposed to protect those forests for future generations.

But to place all the blame on big government and big business is to miss a crucial part of the story. René Dubos's admonition to "think globally and act locally" has served as an effective strategy for conservationists. It has let us concentrate on the battles that could be won, and the results have been remarkable. But at the same time, they have also been insufficient.

The heart of the problem is that the conservation movement has failed to develop a truly national strategy, let alone a global one. It is true that many conservation organizations have developed effective *federal* strategies, with important successes in changing policies for federal lands and promoting federal pollution legislation. But we have not developed a coherent set of national conservation goals, entraining federal, state, and local jurisdictions in coordinated action. We do not have a national consensus about important conservation issues, promoting and guiding mutually supportive action among nonprofit organizations, government, and business. We do not have a shared commitment to conservation well-being, a shared vision of what needs to be done.

To understand both the possibilities and the limits of a national vision, consider the history of education in the United States. Through most of the nineteenth century, children were taught, if at all, in a patchwork of local public and private schools. Then, in the fifty years from 1860 to 1910, universal education became a national priority. It was a difficult transition, with resistance from politicians, businessmen, churches, and parents. But all sectors of society eventually bought in. The system is still far from perfect, and the process far from finished. Yet we do have a national vision. And we do have a national infrastructure that—however loosely and haltingly—ties together local, state, and federal policies. Much educational policy is still set by local citizens acting locally, but they do so in a framework of common standards and values.

The cause of universal education is no longer limited to the movement. It has become the common concern of the nation, of states, and of local communities. Although people will always disagree about goals and methods, they do not disagree that education is an essential concern of society. They share a general vision of the future that is short of hope if education is denied to their children. As members of a community, they do not disagree about the essential importance of education. They assume that they have a right and an obligation to take part in making educational decisions.

Can conservation become a similar national concern? We have reason for hope. For several years, public opinion polls have consistently shown that an overwhelming majority of Americans want a cleaner, healthier environment and are willing to pay for it. The same polls show that conservation issues rank high on the list of problems that most concern Americans. Conservation leaders are by no means powerless, but if they are to take advantage of the opportunities before them, they need to rethink some strategies.

As support for conservation issues has grown, so has the number of conservation organizations. The best directory of conservation organizations in the United States lists almost 3,000 groups. But findings of the Conservation Leadership Project suggest that the actual number may be closer to 10,000. No one really knows how many people are actively involved in conservation, because most of the new groups are small, run by volunteers, and focused on local issues. Yet, ironically, as popular concern about conservation issues has grown and as the number of organizations working on those issues has increased, the conservation movement as a whole has not mobilized that growing, potential support into an effective national force.

Because they are small, local, and underfunded, most conservation organizations are struggling simply to survive. Of all the messages delivered by the questionnaires and interviews of the Conservation Leadership Study, the most poignantly disturbing is the repeated theme of underpaid staff and overcommitted boards and volunteers working too many hours each day to deploy inadequate resources against complex, turbulent issues. Meanwhile, an ever-increasing number of organizations compete for the same thin slice of the pie. Despite recent growth, conservation organizations still enroll only a minuscule percentage of Americans as members and supporters. On Earth Day, twenty years ago, support for conservation causes accounted for about 1 percent of all U.S. philanthropy, and it still does.

As a result, conservation leaders are caught in a chronic scramble for money and administrative stability. According to the Conservation Leadership Study, the average conservation leader spends over 70 percent of his or her time on fund-raising, planning, board development, personnel, membership development, public speaking, and media relations. He allocates less than 29 percent to program implementation and programmatic research, and spends only 2 percent on personal and professional development.

These leaders are like people in a lifeboat with a few days' food and water and no rescue in sight. In such straits, even the most generous begin to ponder the ethics of cannibalism. The result is a version of the tragedy of the commons, in which the rational pursuit of self-interest leads to hardship for all. For example, leaders of nonprofit conservation organizations hoard the names of their best donors as they would the last biscuits on the boat. If self-interest were the only criterion, that would be a rational tactic for survival. But it is patently not best for the movement.

In the past when conservation leaders have attempted to set national goals for the nation as a whole, their pronouncements have fallen mostly on deaf ears. A few years ago, the publisher of this book published such an effort in *A Conservation Agenda for the Future* (Washington, D.C.: Island Press, 1985), in which leaders of ten of the most influential national conservation organizations lent their support to recommendations for action on a diverse set of conservation issues. These men (and significantly, through no fault of their own, they *were* all men) are experienced, accomplished, knowledgeable, hardworking and, in the context of their own organizations, effective. The book contains much useful insight and advice, and it may have influenced debate about some of the issues. In no way, however, did it result in the adoption of a coherent, national "conservation agenda."

The limited impact of the book was not the result of any personal limitations on the part of the authors. Rather, it was the result of two systemic problems. First, the book was an ad hoc effort. There is no permanent infrastructure to truly formulate and promote a unified agenda. No organization or coalition of organizations has persistently set priorities on behalf of the conservation movement as a whole. No organization exists to translate common priorities into coherent, long-term initiatives of legislative policy, scientific research, and economic initiatives, nor to hone those initiatives in the give-and-take of politics, business, and science. In fact, the very idea of having one organization act as the movement's voice would be anathema to many conservation leaders, who would see such a development as a challenge to their own power and a potential threat to their organization's own agenda.

The second problem is that in political terms, the leaders who endorsed the conservation agenda lacked legitimacy. Given their accomplishments and influence, many of them might well have deserved to speak for the movement, but still they were self-anointed. While they were gathering to hammer out their recommendations, thousands of other conservation leaders were oblivious to their efforts, going about the business of saving whatever piece of the environment they had adopted. Those thousands had not asked these ten to speak for them, and we can safely assume that a large portion of those thousands never read the book. Nor was that fact lost on the politicians and bureaucrats whom the ten hoped to influence. To neutralize the conservation movement, it is not necessary to divide and conquer. The movement already *is* divided, and so there is little to conquer.

In 1758 David Hume summed up the situation in *Of the First Principles of Government*:

> Nothing appears more surprising to those who consider human affairs with a philosophical eye than the easiness with which the many are governed by the few, and the implicit submission with which men resign their own sentiments and passions to those of their rulers. When we inquire by what means this wonder is effected, we shall find that, as Force is always on the side of the governed, the governors have nothing to support them but opinion. It is, therefore, on opinion only that government is founded, and this maxim extends to the most despotic and most military governments as well as to the most free and most popular.

When 80 percent of all Americans want real conservation reform and their government drags its heels, we clearly have a cause of the many being governed by the few. And the few have followed Hume's formula. They have used the power of opinion to downplay the issues. Until recently they had persuaded a plurality of voters that organized conservationists were a fringe group. Ronald Reagan was fond of calling conservationists a special interest, as if a lethal environment affected only those who shared certain eccentric obsessions while sparing those who remained silent. Reagan and others also argued that conservation protection required unacceptable trade-offs, raising the fear of lost jobs, brownouts, and underpowered cars.

Meanwhile, they argued that the government really was working on the problem. Laws were, in fact, passed, and sometimes enforced. The media—the government's chief accomplice in opinion management—descended on each newly discovered superfund site with relish. Nothing sells newspapers and boosts TV news ratings like a good scandal, and the media diligently carried pictures of governmental investigators "discovering" acres of rusting drums leaking poisonous chemicals. Fines were levied and billions were appropriated, with more good coverage. That the world was continuing its steady decline despite so much sound and fury was a more depressing and confusing story, and therefore not "immediate" news.

The effect of these uses of opinion was to persuade people that although conservation problems might be real, the ordinary citizen could not (and, if he wanted to be a regular guy, should not) do anything about them. This was a job for experts. No one else could understand the metaphysics of "risk analysis," calculating the exact point at which the net present value of future deaths exceeded the economic cost of controls. And it was a job requiring heavy muscle. Who but government agencies and large corporations could marshal the resources to attack the problems? And so 80 percent of the people continued to worry whether their food and water were safe or whether the natural places they loved would be destroyed or whether their children would have a habitable world. And they continued to hope someone else would take care of the problems.

As we near the end of the century, the United States seems to be in a state of moral paralysis. We face a group of pervasive crises whose gravity we acknowledge but about which we seem incapable of effective action. Thirteen million of our children—one in five—live in poverty. Many of them are children of chemically addicted parents, who are in growing numbers children themselves who receive little help in practicing birth control or child rearing. They learn early that there is apparent escape either by taking drugs or by selling them. To protect themselves, or in pursuit of their criminal vocations, those children buy guns that society insists on making available to them. Money that could be used to help them is siphoned off by a crushing national debt, which is to a large degree fueled by our addiction to redundant weapons systems for national defense.

In all these issues—poverty, drugs, family planning, gun control, and defense policy—the political debate is as much about values, emotions, and attitudes as it is about practical solutions. That is why resolution is so difficult. And the same could be said about conservation issues. The wilderness debate, for example, is about economics, but it is also about something more. Even when solutions are proposed that protect both wilderness and jobs, the battle often rages on.

At times, the wilderness debate seems to reveal an unbridgeable chasm between two kinds of people: those who believe that people have a right and perhaps a duty to inhabit and use all corners of the natural world versus those who believe that nature has an autonomous existence of its own and that we should honor that autonomy.

In fact, however, the debate revolves within each of us. Hardly anyone wants to go without food, shelter, and reliable income. Most of us want a healthy environment, and most find peace and humility in the presence of nonhuman nature. Circumstance and ideology may interfere, but even the most hungry or the most civilized person still wants a quiet place with grass and green trees, and even the most misanthropic wilderness champion still wants a livable society. In the heat of debate, we may repress one or the other impulse, but both are innate and ineradicable.

We are not divided by hopeless differences. We are divided by social and economic systems of our own making. We have built effective systems for economic development, and we have devised laws and policies for environmental protection. We have few systems for pursuing both at the same time. At its deepest the debate is about cultural values, and it can finally be resolved only by a cultural realignment. In its usual guise the debate has no workable resolution. Changing the terms of the debate is the greatest challenge facing American leaders, including leaders of the conservation movement.

Society resolves moral debates by creating institutions. By *institution* I mean any form of organization that objectifies a set of values important to society and serves as society's primary agent in protecting, interpreting, and promoting those values. We usually think of institutions as huge organizations, and some, like the Red Cross or the Catholic church, fit that image. Other institutions, however, may be quite small and decentralized. For example, we have institutionalized our respect for literacy through local public libraries, and we have institutionalized our sexual and familial mores through a complex web of laws, taboos, and expectations surrounding the nuclear family.

Institutions determine individual behavior. People participate in institutions by adopting roles that prescribe how they will act. A judge, for example, may do many things in private life that he or she would not think of doing on the bench, because legal institutions bind judges to a complex code of behavior. When institutions are working well, people internalize their values so thoroughly that they are not aware that they have adopted a role. They are simply doing things "the way they are done." If we had to decide anew every moral dilemma we faced every day, we might prefer to stay in bed. Institutions relieve some of that burden. They teach us how others have acted, and they show us the approved way. Their influence is most powerful when it is least noticed. When other organizations want to influence people's behavior, they have to explain *why* their cause is important. Institutions rarely have that problem.

The challenge facing conservation leaders, especially leaders of nongovernmental organizations, is to institutionalize environmental values so that those values will have equal weight with others, such as the values of commerce and military defense. To do so, conservationists have a choice of two strategies: Either they can induce existing institutions to assimilate environmental values, or they can create institutions in their own right. The first strategy is sometimes easier; the second is more secure. Many organizations can pursue both at the same time.

To employ either strategy, however, many conservation leaders will have to reexamine their own values. We need to build a national vision of environmental well-being, a vision based on consensus. Any attempt to build a vision that does not include government and business, as well as nongovernmental conservation organizations, is doomed from the outset. There, for many conservationists, is where change will be hardest. For conservationists, the central institutions of society have often been not havens but hostile camps. Conservationists have seen themselves as outsiders, people of the borderlands, a tribe perpetually beset by more powerful "others"—say, the Bureau of Reclamation or oil companies or subdividers. Not only do the others have access to power and money, but they actually own a large part of the environment in question. No wonder many conservation leaders spend their days in a state of wary, contentious alienation. Add that attitude to the factious nature of the movement itself, and the hope for a cohesive, institutionalized national vision seems slim.

But we have no choice. If the conservation movement does not overcome its antipathy to collaborative institutional development, it will be overwhelmed. Politicians are taking another look at the public opinion polls, and a growing number of them like what they see. Old reliable campaign issues, such as the Red threat, now play to empty houses. New emotion-laden issues, like abortion, seem politically dangerous no matter what side one takes. By contrast, conservation looks like an easy winner. The year 1988 saw the first presidential election in which the condition of the environment was a major issue, both candidates claiming to be the better environmentalist. Conservation issues will be a part of every national election, and an increasing number of state and local elections, from now on. An official of the Office of Management and Budget, the last bastion of bureaucratic anticonservationism, was recently quoted as saying, "Everyone under forty is an environmentalist."

The greatest danger to the conservation movement is no longer that our government will shun conservation action. To the contrary, our government is likely to smother environmental problems with politics. If we lack institutions with the strength and vision to provide moral leadership, the new money will do some good, but much of it will be squandered on trivial, ineffectual, cosmetic, counterproductive projects. In such times bureaucracy passes for competence, and expediency for wisdom. The danger is that leaders who could help guide events will be unprepared.

To understand what should be done, it is necessary to understand the structure of the conservation movement. It is a pyramid, with many small organizations at the bottom and a few large ones at the top. The organizations within this pyramid are a diverse assortment, and any generalization about them is a gross oversimplification. Still, it is useful to think of the pyramid as consisting of three layers. Organizations in each layer share important characteristics, work in broadly similar institutional environments, and require generally similar qualities of leadership.

Leaders at the lowest layer, where the majority of organizations subsist, are jacks of all trades. Three-fourths of the organizations surveyed by the Conservation Leadership Project have three or fewer full-time paid staff. These organizations come in many models and colors—including land trusts, groups fighting local pollution problems, state and national single-issue organizations, and new organizations with small means and large dreams. Their leaders are usually volunteers, part-timers, or people who have recently moved from other professions. Usually those leaders have little experience in managing a nonprofit organization. More often than not, the leader also founded the organization, and the organization is substantially an extension of his or her personal vision and style. Organizational decisions are personal decisions or the decisions of a small, closely knit group.

Jacks of all trades must be technically competent in all aspects of their programs. The best of them are street-smart, masters at doing much with little. Their working environment is dominated by larger, more powerful institutions, and so they achieve much of their results by using volunteers and influencing public opinion. As a rule, their organizations have a relatively short life expectancy unless they grow to a more stable size. The ones that do survive usually have a leader who personifies a mission, and by the strength of his or her commitment and personality involves others in that quest.

In the middle layer of the pyramid we find leaders whom we may call builders. Their organizations have achieved a measure of stability and recognition. These organizations often have more than one fairly well defined program area. They support annual budgets of (very roughly) $500,000 to $5,000,000 and employ as few as 10 or as many as 100 full-time staff. The typical midsize conservation organization is supported by a handful of major donors—people or foundations— and perhaps by loyal members. It may have precarious cash flow, but it has the organizational self-confidence to look ahead and set long-range goals. It intends to endure. It has struck alliances with other organizations or public agencies, and perhaps with the business world. Its staff includes a few specialists—for example, in conservation law, science, legislation, public relations, publishing, or fundraising—but often not enough to cover the operating programs adequately.

The builders' task is to establish their organization's place in the larger community. They must be especially adept at the arts of strategy, communication, and delegation. They need to set a course that will let the organization advance its mission with the least interference and the most support from both insiders and outsiders. To do so, they need to understand a complex working environment and the strengths and weaknesses of their own organization. They need to be able to communicate goals persuasively to a wide variety of audiences, including the specialists in their organization who may be inclined to focus on their own careers or their own departments rather than the good of the organization. They need to set objectives for subordinates that will use their strengths and let them stretch to the maximum. And they need to be generalists who can evaluate the performance of their staff validly and objectively. They need to inspire the whole organization through their own competence, reliability, perseverance, fairness, and vision.

The third layer of conservation organizations is those with budgets in the tens of millions of dollars and relatively large staffs. There are only about fifty such organizations, roughly 0.1 percent of all conservation organizations in the United States. Yet they wield influence far greater than their number. The majority have headquarters in national centers of power such as New York City, Washington, D.C., or San Francisco. Often they have multiple field offices, and so they have a national as well as a federal presence.

The leaders of the Big 50—call them guardians—are quoted on the wire services, testify before Congress, and endorse books about national agendas. They act as the guardians of national conservation values. Most guardians are sincerely committed to effective national action. But if they lack vertical lines of communication to the lower layers of the pyramid, they are also fatally out of touch with those they hope to lead. Even when they do try to communicate and listen, they are still captives of their own organizational goals and needs, with more incentive to compete than to collaborate. Lacking formal means of ongoing communication, they rarely work with the other layers of the pyramid.

Although the guardians' field staffs could help, structural problems within the largest organizations often prevent reports from the front from being heard at headquarters. Many of these organizations have grown too fast, with little or no planning. Some are overly centralized, whereas others are so decentralized that they are torn by factions and internal fiefdoms. In either case, national-level decisions are made without reliable information. Consumed by fund-raising and their own work on national issues—and in many cases untrained in management—guardians often lack the time or the tools to correct their dysfunctional organizations.

With a pyramid of such diversity and fragmentation, it is fair to ask whether there is a single conservation movement and whether the idea of a national consensus is a quixotic pipe dream. If there is hope, it does not lie in forcing the movement to be more homogenous. In fact, we need even more diversity. For example, the nascent movement in which inner-city residents are beginning to attack inner-city environmental problems needs to grow and develop its own inner-city strategies. The conservation movement is diverse, even messy, for good reasons. Its goals and issues are diverse. It operates in a diversity of working environments. And since those environments are turbulent and fluid, it is necessarily opportunistic, responding to new problems and opportunities with new tactics and organizations. Those organizations may be makeshift, and they may not always work well, but they have an entrepreneurial vitality that is potentially a well of renewal and enduring, resourceful strength.

The conservation movement should seek not unity but community. Disparate movements throughout the pyramid can collaborate while maintaining separate identities, but only to the extent that collaboration is based on mutual respect and a constant flow of reliable information.

Conservation leaders need to foster such collaboration, and not only with each other. They need to reach out beyond those few million people who already have multiple memberships in conservation organizations. That will require new methods of recruitment besides trading direct-mail lists with like-minded groups. It will require research, planning, and committed action to find out who those potential supporters are, what they want, and how to meet those wants with integrity. It will require alliances with business, labor, civil rights groups, recreationists, service clubs, neighborhood associations, hospitals, law enforcement groups, churches, and anyone else with the common sense to recognize common ground. It will require changing some deep habits of territoriality, class distinctions, and suspicion. If they succeed, conservation leaders will enlarge the vision and implant the values of conservation where they belong, in the everyday soul of American endeavors.

Although the differences among organizations are here to stay, the obstacles to common action can be circumvented. If Congress or national foundations want to spend a little money for large effect, they can do two things. First, they can support efforts by existing organizations to improve their own internal functioning and development so that those organizations can determine their most important goals and spend less energy achieving them. Mundane instruments such as strategic planning and management information systems are crucial tools lacking in most conservation organizations. Without those tools, organizations cannot hope to see opportunities, set priorities, understand and cooperate with each other, interact effectively with other institutions, or learn from their mistakes and successes.

Second, funders can subsidize organizations and programs designed to consolidate the movement. These would be intermediary organizations, deliberately designed to build bridges and carry messages between disparate groups. They would not attempt to span the whole movement but would have expertise in broad categories of environmental issues—such as toxic chemicals, land conservation, industrial or agricultural production, or population ecology. That expertise would give them the credibility and judgment to facilitate coalitions and keep their part of the community informed about each others' doings.

Such outreach will pay off throughout the pyramid. Smaller organizations need not aspire to join the Big 50 in order to contribute to the institutionalization of conservation values. On the contrary, any organization can become an institution in its own environment. Too often, the problem is not that the organization is too small but that it has a vague mission or has not identified its constituencies or has not recognized opportunities or has not used its strengths effectively. Most conservation issues are local issues, and most supporters of conservation causes have parochial concerns. Even the smallest organization has a chance to be supported by a grateful constituency.

We have two obstacles to framing a cohesive vision: the differences in style, structure, goals, and working environment among conservation groups and the insularity of conservation organizations within society as a whole. Overcoming those obstacles is a function of leadership. Anyone at any level in an organization can be a leader. Anyone who is the head of an organization, a staff or board member, or a volunteer can help institutionalize the conservation movement.

If you are such a leader, you can find opportunities to take any of the following six steps:

1. *Become obsessed with communication.* Look for or create opportunities to communicate laterally and vertically with other leaders. Support newsletters or journals for other organizations with similar interests, or start one yourself. By communicating better with other leaders, a leader can communicate better with the public. He or she will not only become more of an expert, but will have a better feel for what issues mean to supporters. Listen to those supporters and find out what they really expect of you. Survey them and talk to them. Ask them what they do *not* like about your organization, and understand that their complaints are opportunities for learning and adapting. Perhaps the most common mistake conservation organizations make is to assume that since their cause is just, everyone else will support it. And if you do not know how the media really work or how to make a speech, learn. Then work the media and make speeches every chance you get.

2. *Create, support, and take advantage of opportunities for leadership training.* The qualities of conservation leaders are at base the qualities of all leaders: creativity, a bias toward seeing the whole rather than parts, strategic thinking, confidence in one's own judgment, the ability to understand others, an understanding of one's own strengths and weaknesses, a breadth of knowledge beyond one's own specialty, the ability to find common ground

between one's own vision and the aspirations of others, the ability to express the vision persuasively, and an indomitable loyalty to the vision. Many of these qualities can be learned.

3. *Think strategically.* Start by asking these questions: (1) What can your organization do that is useful for people as well as for the natural world? What services can it provide that others want and will therefore support? How can you sharpen your goals so that you are still achieving your conservation mission while meeting other people's needs? (2) What can you do that is unique? If you are doing something that another organization is also doing, then one of you should change or get out of the way. The alternative is a future of continually trying to outhustle each other, with frustratingly small results. You want your organization to be an institution, and institutions are by definition unique. That is one reason they are indispensable. (3) What can you do to establish the highest standards of quality? Analyze your strengths and resources, and decide how to deploy them to act with excellence. (4) How can you become recognized for doing something useful, unique, and excellent? What audiences do you need to reach for support? How can you reach them, consistently and persistently, so that your good works are known and appreciated?

4. *Act for the movement.* Share what you have learned with leaders of other organizations. Turn competitors into collaborators. Believe that you gain power by sharing it. Become a mentor, and you will strengthen both the movement and your own organization. Organize the movement by organizing your peers. Arrange summit meetings—local, state, regional, national—to which participants come expecting to create common agendas and workable, permanent vehicles for promoting those agendas. Make room in your already spare budget for that kind of action.

5. *Broaden the movement by broadening your organization.* If your supporters include few people from ethnic minorities, few women, or few poor people, find out why. By all means, look for ways to bring them in, such as internships and other recruiting tac-

tics. But understand that the challenge is not to make other people more like you, because that will not work for most people. Your challenge is to change your organization so that it really is serving the needs of your community, state, or nation in the broadest way possible consistent with your mission. There is a multiplier effect as you broaden your constituency. If the next 10 percent you add to your membership comes from a new segment of the population, you will increase your political power by much more than 10 percent.

6. *Broaden your organization by striking new kinds of alliances.* As conservation issues become everyone's concern, look for common ground with the "others." Everyone has a role to play. Business contributes technical expertise and decisions about the use of natural resources. Government contributes societal goals and coordination. Nonprofits contribute a concern for externalities, education, and vision. As ecological values become more central, so will the role of organizations not specifically dedicated to conservation action. Successful nonprofits will be those that know how to make their contributions collaboratively, and how to do what government and business cannot or should not do.

The notion that conservation progress requires organizational savvy contradicts one of the most hallowed images of conservationism: the image of the visionary and charismatic leader striding alone beneath the stars, or chained to a dozer. The conservation movement has been inspired by individual people who made a difference—John Muir, Gifford Pinchot, Bob Marshall, Aldo Leopold, Rachel Carson. They were prophets and saints of the movement. Among those of us who follow, each name evokes an idea that reordered the world. However, we often lose sight of the fact that each of them was a catalyst for groups that survived them. They saw the need for action, and in answering that need, they gave purpose to organizations. In a complex society that conducts its affairs through the give-and-take of institutions, there is no other way.

To develop and implement a conservation agenda for all Americans, existing organizations must be strengthened and new organizations must be created to fill the gaps now existing. That is the task of leadership. Conservation leaders tend to see themselves as issues people first and organization builders second. Repeatedly, leaders have told the Conservation Leadership Project of their frustration in spending too much time on organizational management and fund-raising. Time spent attending to those matters, they say, is time spent away from the issues. But the distinction between working on issues and working on organizational effectiveness is a false one. When properly understood and employed, every minute spent working on organizational effectiveness can be a minute spent advancing the cause. For a conservation leader in the late twentieth century, the organization is the only tool available. The leader carries the vision. The organization supplies the voice.

2 The Conservation Movement as a Political Force

NATHANIEL P. REED
President, 1000 Friends of Florida

AS A POLITICAL force, the conservation movement manifests a steady pattern from its inception in the late nineteenth century to its heyday in the aftermath of Earth Day 1970 and beyond: the percolation of ideas from local volunteers up to state or national lawmakers and policymakers. There have been exceptions to this directional movement—of necessity during the Reagan presidency, more initiatives remained at the local level than previously—but as a generality it holds true. American conservation is a process of bringing problems first perceived in one's neighborhood to the attention of those with the political power required to solve them.

John Muir himself was involved in a classic situation. In his last campaign, the one to save Hetch Hetchy Valley in Yosemite National Park from being dammed to provide water for the city of San Francisco, Muir was, as always, the volunteer pitted against the professionals. In this case the movement from local to national level was guaranteed because the secretary of the interior had to approve any tampering with park resources. But the impetus behind the challenge to the city's scheme was strictly local: It came from Muir's Sierra Club, which in those days was still an organization composed almost entirely of Californians.

Historian Stephen Fox has sketched the lineup of players in the conflict in his book *John Muir and His Legacy: The American Conservation Movement*. Granted that sincere conservationists should disagree about the project, the real division was not between utilitarians and preservationists. Rather, it was occupational, between those who urged the dam *as part of their jobs* and those who *took time from their jobs* to oppose it. In short, another collision of professionals and amateurs. The dam's prime movers were politicians from the San Francisco area—where public opinion overwhelmingly called for the dam—and engineers and consultants hired by the city. All had a professional stake in pushing the project through. Their opponents, by contrast, had to steal time from their livelihoods. "We are all persons of small means and we have made considerable sacrifice," the Sierra Club's William Colby noted. "The city has employed experts and skilled attorneys at an expense of thousands of dollars because it has a personal advantage to be gained. The fight has been a most unequal one from this standpoint." Ultimately, Muir and company lost that fight; but they had already won a good many others that followed the same pattern of evolution—from the agendas and petitions of grassroots volunteers to the in-boxes of governmental decision makers.

Incidentally, Colby's lament gives the lie to the widespread belief that the conservation movement has been dominated by elitists—rich dilettantes who could bankroll their own participation. To be sure, elitists have enrolled in conservation campaigns. Acadia National Park would not exist if it hadn't been for the backing of two men of means, Charles W. Eliot and George B. Dorr, and one genuine plutocrat, John D. Rockefeller, Jr. And the National Audubon Society's admirable system of refuges originated with a fund created by philanthropist Abbott Thayer in 1900. But by and large, conservationists have come from the middle class—like Colby, like Muir. During the golden age of the environmental movement, the decade from 1966 to 1975, five major conservation groups—the Izaak Walton League, the National Audubon Society, the National Wildlife Federation, the Sierra Club, and the Wilderness Society—enjoyed a collective tripling of their membership. These hundreds of thousands of new members tended to be not elitists who had already heard the conservationists' appeals and responded to them in one way or another, but middle-class people who were hearing the message for the first time.

The Muir model crops up again and again throughout conservation history. The Tropic Everglades National Park Association was founded in 1928 by a Miami businessman. Six years later the group's efforts bore fruit in the law establishing Everglades National Park. Jumping to the 1970s, we find that the New River Valley in North Carolina was spared from a hydroelectric dam thanks largely to the efforts of the valley's residents and landowners. They took their case to Washington, enlisted their formidable senator, Sam Ervin, and eventually prevailed upon Congress to cancel the Federal Power Commission's license to dam.

The Save the Redwoods League provides an example of keeping the action at the state level—but only after an appeal to the feds was not heard. Established in 1918 to preserve the big trees, the league originally set its sights on a national park. When Congress did not rush to embrace the idea, the league decided to approach the state. This redeployment of force resulted in the establishment of several state parks that are recognized today as the gems of the California system. Decades later, when it became clear that the state parks were threatened by logging outside their boundaries and that only a protected zone embracing the major watershed along which the trees grow could ensure their survival, the idea of a redwoods national park was revived; such a park was established in 1968, amid great controversy and with strong regional support in the face of opposition by the timber industry.

This, then, has been the pattern for hundreds of conservation initiatives over the years. You have a legislature or governmental agency only dimly aware of an issue that may be a burning cause for those who live near the affected area. You have local residents who organize and set about raising the governmental consciousness. If they articulate their position well and the political winds are with them, they succeed in establishing the park or refuge or wilderness area they want, or blocking the development project or pollution source they don't want.

I don't mean to say that the lawmakers and executives didn't take the initiative some of the time. Indeed, they did. President Theodore Roosevelt established the first federal wildlife refuge by executive order in 1903 and called the first national conference on the environment in 1909. Harold Ickes, Franklin Roosevelt's secretary of the interior, was instrumental in the establishment of Olympic and Kings Canyon national parks and Jackson Hole National Monument.

Some of the best work in the annals of conservation has been done by those with a foot in both camps—savvy insiders or former insiders who used experience gained from government service to make an impact from the outside. The wilderness concept can be traced to Aldo Leopold, who, while working for the U.S. Forest Service, urged the idea upon his superiors. Among the first wilderness areas set aside (by administrative order—this was long before the Wilderness Act) was one in the Gila National Forest, where Leopold was stationed at the time. After leaving government service in 1924, he worked assiduously to inculcate what he called a "land ethic" in the nation as a whole.

The consummate example of someone who applies expertise gained in the course of government service to set change in motion from the outside is Rachel Carson. After toiling as a writer and editor for the predecessor to today's U.S. Fish and Wildlife Service in the 1940s and 1950s, she quit to write full-time. A friend brought to her attention the connection between the spraying of the pesticide DDT and the decline in American bird populations, and she went to work. From her untrammeled position in private life, Carson didn't have to worry about offending any of her former colleagues or flouting administration policy (the Agriculture Department not only approved of the chemical's use; in some cases it did the spraying itself). The result was *Silent Spring,* a book that galvanized the nation's conscience as few others have. DDT was eventually banned, and the Toxic Substances Control Act of 1976 set up a mechanism for ensuring that such a blunder will not be made again.

On a more modest level, my own career exhibits the same insider-outsider dynamic. When I took over as assistant secretary of the interior for fish, wildlife, and parks, I brought along with me a keen interest in Florida and its environmental problems, some of which I had worked on in Governor Claude Kirk's administration. When proposals such as the construction of a jetport in Florida, the development of March Island, and the digging of a cross-Florida barge canal came across my desk, I addressed them both with an insider's knowledge and a former local conservationist's passion. I played fair, and certainly I never profited financially from any of the environmental work other than drawing a federal paycheck from 1971 to 1977. But I entered each of these Florida frays with a distinct advantage: As former Speaker of the House Tip O'Neill once declared, "All politics is local."

I gave my staff members enough flexibility to pursue their own pet issues. One of my deputies had gone to law school in North Carolina, and the campaign to save the New River profited immensely from his informed pleas on its behalf. One of my special assistants grew up in St. Louis and concerned himself with the Corps of Engineers' proposed dam on the nearby Meramec River. We were able to make more knowledgeable cases for saving such places because we knew them intimately. We had canoed the rivers, walked the trails. It was in our capacity as former outsiders to make an extra contribution once we became insiders.

At the same time that committed conservationists have been turning up on the federal payroll, conservation organizations have been busy accumulating enough expertise to challenge the government on its own turf: the use and interpretation of statistics. Periodically, amateurs had tried to contest the government's figures, with little success. A famous exception involved David Brower of the Sierra Club, who once shocked a congressional hearing by torpedoing the Bureau of Reclamation's cost-benefit analysis. His double-checking of the bureau's arithmetic forced it to whittle down the projected water-saving superiority of the proposed Echo Park dam site in Dinosaur National Monument over other possible sites to one-tenth the original estimate. The dam was not built. But at the time the Sierra Club had no economists on staff to do this kind of analysis as a matter of course, and Brower himself—still going strong in his late seventies—may be the last of the great amateur environmentalists. At least this much seems certain: The Sierra Club will never again hire as its executive director a man who, like Brower, dropped out of college in his sophomore year.

In contrast, today's complete conservation organization is well-stocked with professionals: wildlife biologists, economists, attorneys, natural resource specialists of every stripe. Their fact collecting and number crunching are so sophisticated that they have the capacity to call entire federal programs into question. The Wilderness Society has recently done just that with its carefully supported allegation that no matter how you slice it, timber cutting in the national forests is a money-losing proposition. To reach this conclusion, the society spent several person-years on a comprehensive study of the forests—an indication of how conservation groups have broadened their field of play from ad hoc efforts to save this or prevent that. Similarly, the Worldwatch Institute's annual *State of the World* report offers more complete and meaningful coverage of its subject than anything the federal government produces.

While conservation groups have been busy staffing up, the states have become full participants in the process. Most states had decent park systems in place by the 1960s, but since Earth Day many of these systems have grown exponentially, some of them funded by tax-return checkoffs—an innovation pioneered by the state of Missouri. And where once there were only state parks, we now find a whole spectrum of land and water protection categories at the state level: wildlife refuges, wild and scenic rivers, and trails. Fifty-one states and territories now have their own versions of the most controversial federal protection program, the one to list and save endangered plant and animal species.

Within some states, significant environmental expertise has accumulated at the regional level. In Alameda and Contra Costa counties, across the bay from San Francisco, the parks movement was born more than fifty years ago in a Depression-era bond issue. From that beginning has grown the East Bay Regional Park District's superb roster of parks, trails, and shorelines. Its managers have developed enough expertise and self-confidence to undertake a tricky program: reintroduction of the tule elk, a species that once flourished in the region but died out there with the encroachment of civilization.

In my home state, a state agency, the South Florida Water Management District, has embarked on an even more complex project: returning the Kissimmee River to its natural state. The Corps of Engineers got hold of the river in the 1960s and perverted its meandering, habitat-entrenching course into an arrow-straight ditch, the kind of result that brings tears of joy to an engineer's eyes but sends storks flying for cover. After living with this mistake for a generation, Floridians—led by that formidable grande dame of conservation Marjorie Stoneman Douglas—decided they wanted their river back. With the help of a University of California professor who has built an eighty-by-sixty-foot model of a river mile in his lab near the Berkeley campus, the district is nearing completion of the project's first phase, the restoration of a twelve-mile stretch. If you keep in mind that what you have here is a district arm of Florida's state water agency unraveling the work of the U.S. Army and that no one has ever before applied civil engineering techniques to undo environmental harm wrought by civil engineering itself, you can see that some states are moving into the very forefront of environmental expertise.

They're also finding the political will to accomplish things that the federal government is still only talking about. George Bush's campaign pledge "No New Loss of Wetlands" is already a reality in New Jersey, where a program to ensure exactly that was set up under the leadership of then Governor Kean. States like California, Minnesota, and Maine have passed bond issues to raise money needed for the orderly acquisition of key natural resource properties, while the feds still make do with a jerry-built and undependable system drawing on the Land and Water Conservation Fund. State and local governments and conservation organizations have become fertile laboratories for ideas and approaches, and if you want to know where conservation leadership exists today, take a nationwide tour of state capitals.

The management of the subfederal network of land, water, and wildlife, of these highly sophisticated projects, requires professionals, and the professionalization of the conservation community may be the most profound change in the way we do business that I've seen in my time. It was beginning to happen when I started working in Washington. High schools and colleges were starting to teach environmental courses, and law schools were assembling courses on the new laws being passed. By now some of the students in those early classes have themselves become teachers of environmental subjects, and the movement survives as much through them as it does via mailed appeals and magazine ads.

Speaking of those appeals, the conservation groups could not have hired such highly educated people to direct such ambitious projects without growth. It has been estimated that today there are amost 12,000 conservation and outdoors groups, and the major national conservation groups have a combined membership of 7 million. This position has been attained by a combination of skill, luck, zeitgeist, and old-fashioned mail campaigning, and the foremost of these, I'm afraid, has been the old-fashioned one.

I would never be presumptuous enough to criticize a group for restoring to these periodic dunning letters, but I do think that too heavy a reliance on them undermines that sense of community that is one of the strengths of the environmental movement. Such coalitions of citizens are important expressions of democracy—de Tocqueville praised them as singularly American institutions in his *Democracy in America*—and they may perform an accentuated safety-valve function in a society where enormousness—of the country, of the problems it faces, of the difficulty in finding money to spend on making improvements—can make us all feel that our votes are more of a religious ritual than a meaningful political act.

There was a time when it took more than just a check to become a member of the Sierra Club: You needed a sponsor from within the club. Granted, this approach smacks too much of fraternity rushing to be viable now, but I'm not sure it's worse than a relationship that is consummated in the mailbox. Conservation groups—that is, their staffs—need to develop better methods for involving their membership in the organization's business, or at least in the resources they are trying to preserve. To stick with the Sierra Club, it has long offered such opportunities in its annual highlight trips; these are open to all members and are ballyhooed each year in a special issue of the club's magazine. By taking such trips to the backcountry, Sierrans can refresh their spirits and remind themselves of what they were hoping to save when they wrote that membership check. Without such opportunities, conservation groups may become mere aggregates of people who have simply answered the same appeal letter and read the same newsletter or magazine put out every few months by the group's journalists clear across the country.

But more troubling than the possible estrangement of members from their conservation groups is, to borrow a phrase from Barry Commoner, the closing circle of the American environmental community. With almost everyone a certified professional—and very likely one who has worked for both the government and the private sector—aren't we in some danger of cutting ourselves off from the most fertile source of ideas and initiatives throughout our history: impassioned gadfly citizens?

When I was at Interior, my staff and I had to put up with chronic letter writers, phone callers, and in-person visitors who made perfect pests of themselves. Some of them were cranks, some were little old ladies in tennis shoes (though now that everyone wears tennis shoes, why should that matter?). But some of them had good ideas, and I'm sure I did a better job because of their persistence. What they lacked most of all, as a group, was political savvy. They wanted me, one assistant secretary out of six in my department, to pick up a baton, raise my arms, and conduct all three branches of the federal government to their tune.

And yet isn't that exactly the place where this self-reassuring professionalism tends to cause the most complacency? Something becomes politically impossible because all of us in the loop—the administration officials, the Hill staffers, the environmental lobbyists—talk to each other and agree that it's out of bounds. Sometimes it takes an outsider, even a flake, to remind us that there is no virtue in failing even to try.

Since leaving government service I've had a few regrets, but not about things I did. I'm bothered by what I left undone because I thought it would be too unconventional, what I left unsaid because I thought it would sound too rash.

Let me tell you about one of those missed opportunities. After President Ford lost the 1976 election, my staff and I put together a proposal for him to leave office with a flurry of withdrawals under the Antiquities Act of 1906. That law permits the president to set aside federal lands as national monuments for their scientific value and is otherwise open-ended. At the time the Alaska park and refuge proposals had been pending for several years but had seen very little action. The centerpiece of our proposal was a wholesale withdrawal of these areas. A bold plan, admittedly; and in the face of Congress's legislative role, a brazen one. But it would have allowed Gerald Ford to go into glorious retirement as one of the most dynamic conservationists in the history of the presidency and might well have galvanized Congress to pass a more comprehensive Alaska National Interest Lands Conservation Act than the one that finally appeared in 1980.

At any rate, our proposal first encountered the naysayers at the Office of Management and Budget, who tried to kill it with questions. But we found a way around them (the consummate professionals) and began working with the vice-president's staff. At the eleventh hour, however, the word came back, "No go." Ford was on vacation in Aspen, and his staff decided he needed his rest too badly to be confronted with such a breathtaking proposal. I fumed—Ford would have the remainder of his life to catch up on rest if he needed it—but I did nothing. In hindsight, I wish I had pushed harder and earlier, and maybe even leaked the idea to the press. (Ironically, sometimes that is the only way to get a president's attention.) In short, I wish I had been a bit of a crank. By way of a bipartisan footnote, let me add that when President Carter—on the recommendation of Interior Secretary Cecil Andrus—took almost the very action we had urged upon Ford in order to spur Congress to pass an Alaska lands bill, the memo we prepared in 1976 resurfaced as a cornerstone of their legal support.

Let me not be heard as a voice from the past calling for the return of a golden age when conservationists were brilliant amateurs who could outfox the government because God was on their side. If there ever was such a time, it is gone, irretrievably. We cannot do without the professionalism that so many environmental groups have worked so hard to acquire. On the other hand, we should be loathe to drive out all of the good generalists from our midst and even more careful not to cut ourselves off from the notions submitted by people with no claim to environmental expertise other than their concern for that special spot they know and love and want to save. All the professionalism in the world is no match for that kind of informed commitment.

3 Groping Our Way Toward an Environmental Ethic

JOANNA D. UNDERWOOD
President, INFORM, Inc.

As I SAT down to begin writing this essay, I opened my *New York Times* and read "Two-Legged Rogues Are on the Run," a story about elephant poachers in Kenya:

> With the skyrocketing value of ivory, the easy availability of weapons for poachers and the financial inability of fragile African economies to combat the poachers, the elephant population in Africa has been halved in the last ten years. . . . The number has plummeted from 1.3 million to 750,000, with the largest population in Zaire. At the present rate of decline, the elephant will disappear from the continent within ten years.

How does this relate to the issues addressed by the environmental research organization I run—issues involving industrial toxic waste and municipal solid waste? Very closely, it seems to me. Where there is money to be made selling goods, where sophisticated technologies exist to use if not plunder resources, and where the public commitment and necessary funds are not up to the task of restraining the damage, those precious resources—whether animal and plant life, land or the minerals beneath it, pure air or clear water—are being damaged and lost.

It is certainly not just elephants that we, the "two-legged rogues," are decimating in our headlong rush to "progress." In the United States and around this planet, each example of degradation relates more and more to the whole. The issue now is clear: how to sustain life on this planet.

The understanding of the scale of damage caused by humans to the animals, plants, and natural resources in both industrialized and developing nations has risen dramatically in the last twenty years as efforts to monitor the impacts of our activities have expanded. What is being learned is awesome. For example:

- Biologists Anne and Paul Ehrlich, in their book *Extinction* (1981), predict that we may cause the extinction of over 20 percent of all animal and plant species on earth in just the next eleven years. These losses will occur not just from killing animals for pelts and tusks, but from the destruction of tropical forests and other habitats.
- Lester Brown, in his 1987 Worldwatch report *State of the World,* points to the steady loss of soil by wind and water, a rate of erosion now exceeding the rate of soil formation on one-third of the world's farmlands. In the United States alone, we are losing some 4 billion tons of topsoil each year.
- There is an increasing loss of the planet's forest cover from land clearing for agriculture, fuelwood, and building in developing countries, as well as from damage caused by acid rain and other forms of air pollution, the by-products of industrialization. Billions of trees are disappearing, and the results are ominous. Trees serve as the world's primary oxygen bank. Their roots hold soil together and retain moisture, slowing the rate of erosion and runoff.
- The world's very climate and atmosphere are now at risk due to the massive buildup of carbon dioxide as a result of fossil fuel burning combined with deforestation. The Worldwatch Institute's current figure reports an atmospheric increase of 30 percent in carbon dioxide emissions in the last 125 years.
- Along with these global impacts has come an outpouring of chemical wastes from the burgeoning activities of the organic chemical industry in the United States and other industrialized countries. These toxic and hazardous wastes are being injected, poured, and discharged into land, water, and air, creating future risks to health and natural resources.

The dramatic learning curve about the state of our world's environment has been the product of an environmental movement that sprang into existence with the passionate celebration of Earth Day 1970. This national celebration was based on a commitment to a new "environmental ethic" dedicated to preserving the earth's resources and species and to learning to live with them in a sustainable fashion.

Over the last twenty years, while learning much about the environmental problems confronting the nation and the planet, a great variety of conservation organizations have emerged. They have marshaled tremendous energies and diverse skills into the tasks of environmental protection: from scientific, technological, and institutional research to public policy analysis, lobbying and litigating, and local environmental and grass-roots campaigns.

At the same time, a growing body of philosophers, social scientists, academic writers, and theologians have begun assessing the implications of human behavior in religious and ethical terms.

Strangely, the paths of these loose alliances, both committed to a sustainable life on this "small, fragile, spaceship earth," have barely crossed. It is certainly time for this to change. These groups need to share their knowledge and their visions for the future. The history of the last twenty years makes clear that without a deeper commitment to the concept of a worldwide environmental ethic, it will be virtually impossible to harness the technological, economic, or political resources needed to achieve a sustainable way of living.

What do we mean by the term *environmental ethic*? What have the last twenty years taught us that makes the question of ethics so important now? And, finally, what can conservation leaders do to promote more effectively the ethical values needed to accomplish the necessary changes in human activity?

The Environmental Ethic

The environmental ethic that lies at the base of today's environmental movement is different from the conservation ethic voiced at the beginning of this century. As Roderick Nash points out in *The Rights of*

Nature (1989), the early-twentieth-century conservationists such as Gifford Pinchot, the first chief of the U.S. Forest Service, had quite another vision. Their goal was the efficient and wise use of natural resources to best serve mankind's needs. Their philosophy lay behind the vast dam-building activities of the Bureau of Reclamation in the West and the timber-harvesting programs of the Forest Service.

The environmental ethic that has come to the fore in the last twenty years rests on the concept of respecting natural resources and species other than our own and actually according them the same rights to be protected and sustained as those accorded to our species.

This concept contrasts *anthropocentrism,* keeping man at the center of things and as the measure of all values, with *biocentrism,* seeing humans, other species, and natural resources as parts of a planetary life system, with each life-form reliant on and worthy of the respect of others.

This environmental ethic in the United States reaches back to the writings of Henry David Thoreau (1817–1862) and John Muir (1838–1914). Both lived in natural surroundings and wrote fervently about the human species as part of the larger community of life and the importance of a mutually enhancing bond between man and nature not only to enrich human life but also to assure the continuance of life itself. John Muir wrote in 1876: "Why should man value himself as more than a small part of the one great unit of creation?"

The views of Thoreau and Muir echoed the expressions of man's place in awesome nature that have sprung from ethical and religious traditions around the world for centuries. They have come from the Buddhists, with their view of our belonging to the earth; their knowledge that if it were not for the rocks, soil, trees, clouds, and countless sentient beings, we would not be here at all; and their related search for egolessness. They have come from the Shinto tradition in Japan of seeing God in everything—hence the need for profound reverence for all things. In our own country they have arisen in the views of Native Americans whose diverse stories and beliefs affirm the existence of a living spirit in all of nature.

Since Thoreau and Muir sounded the call for an environmental ethic, a growing body of writers, theologians, and philosophers have admonished people against their anthropocentric views and the life-styles that wreak havoc on the world.

Rachel Carson in *Silent Spring* (1962) described eloquently the damage to the North American continent from chemical poisoning and the expanding use of chemical pesticides. Her book was dedicated to Albert Schweitzer, who in 1915 expressed the straight-forward idea that people must restrain themselves or they would destroy the earth. The conclusion of *Silent Spring* summarized Rachel Carson's warning. "The control of nature," she wrote, "is a phrase conceived in arrogance born of the Neanderthal age of biology and philosophy when it was supposed that nature existed for the convenience of man." She proposed instead a "reasonable accommodation" between insects and people; ethics, as a restraining device on technological man, was a means to that end.

Theodore Roszak in *Where the Wasteland Ends* (1972) traced the development of urban industrialized society from agricultural times and noted what he also saw as a growing arrogance in man's ability to control, mold, use, and improve the world. He also pointed to the increasing alienation of man from nature.

Thomas Berry, a prolific writer on environmental ethics and director of the Riverdale Center for Religious Research in New York, has looked at the evolution of recent scientific knowledge, which has revealed the extent to which human activity has harmed the resources that have sustained human life and made it rich and varied. He suggests that the urgency of that knowledge must lead us to a "biocentric ethic" if we want to keep our planet intact.

In his essay "The Viable Human" (1988), Berry writes: "The human community presently has such an exaggerated and even pathological fixation on its own comfort and convenience that it is willing to exhaust any and all of the earth's resources to satisfy its own cravings."

In another essay, Berry discusses the shortsighted interpretation of economics that has led us astray. It is worth quoting at length:

> The human was brought into being by the natural world and can only be sustained by that same world. The first obligation of any economic sys-

tem is to see that the earth system itself is sustained in its abundance and fertility. The well-being of the earth is a condition for the well-being of the human. [Yet] the entire study of economics is cast in terms of national or international economics[;] the great economic advance is supposedly our coming into a comprehensive sense of international or global economy. This term is a falsification since what is really meant is a global "human" economy. There is not the slightest reference to a truly global or planetary economy which would refer to the comprehensive economy of the planet earth itself. Only now, through the efforts of the Worldwatch Institute, World Resources Institute and the Conservation Foundation have we come to an audit of the planet's resources in any comprehensive manner, or to any significant evaluation of what is happening in the larger realm of our industrial economics.

We refer to a national debt of $2.4 billion, to a foreign debt of some $380 million, to a third-world debt due to the United States of some hundreds of billions that is unlikely ever to be paid. Add to these the annual budgetary deficit of some $140 billion. Why is there no reference to the debt due to the earth? The earth is the ultimate guarantor of all debts. When the earth goes into deficit, this should ring a thousand alarms throughout the entire range of our industrial, commercial, and financial establishments.

Looking for Answers in the Last Twenty Years

Born of the ground swell of ethical concern expressed through Earth Day, the modern environmental movement involved millions of American adults and schoolchildren. With the passage of the first national environmental protection laws at about the same time, the United States government made a commitment to protect its land, water, and air resources. The laws passed to enforce this commitment now stand as one of the great legacies of the early environmental movement: the National Environmental Policy Act, which created the U.S. Environmental Protection Agency; the Clean Water Act; the Clean Air Act; and others.

What did we see then as the main challenges? We saw streets and parks filling up with litter. We saw air dark and yellow from soot, sulfur dioxide, and nitrogen oxide emissions pouring from factories and from the tail pipes of millions of cars, buses, and trucks. The

Cuyahoga River in Ohio, bursting into flames from the oily discharges of industry, and Lake Erie, dying from industrial wastes and a choking load of phosphates, became symbols of our environmental degradation.

Over 10,000 schools and 2,000 colleges and universities joined in the Earth Day celebration with nature walks, litter cleanups, and teach-ins on pollution. Looking at the years since 1970, many important lessons emerge as we turn to the future. We learned that

1. the environmental problems we confront are infinitely more complex than we imagined in 1970.
2. the solutions we sought, largely involving pollution-control technical fixes, have had much less success than hoped for.
3. while we have become more aware of our environmental dilemma, our actions suggest that we have a long way to go in fully accepting and acting on the meaning of an environmental ethic.

1970s Environmental Perspective

How comforting it was back in 1970 to believe that our new Environmental Protection Agency and the state environmental bodies created to implement national laws and standards could produce air fit for all to breathe safely by 1975 and "zero discharge of pollutants" into our waterways by 1977. The new EPA quickly set standards for such primary air pollutants as particulates, sulfur dioxides, nitrogen oxides, carbon monoxide and hydrocarbons, and pollutants affecting acidity and biochemical oxygen demand in waterways. But there was little awareness of the far-greater threats that we have come to recognize today.

We had not, for example, grappled with the thousands of toxic chemicals whose level of danger to humans and the environment could not be scientifically verified, making it difficult to establish regulatory standards. We hadn't considered the question of long-range transport of pollutants, particularly SO_x and NO_x, which undergo chemical changes while moving through the atmosphere and fall to the ground as acid precipitation that threatens the life of far-distant lakes and forests. Nor did we recognize the global nature of these threats: that discharges from U.S. fossil-fuel power plants and copper smelters could cause acid rain damage in Canada, or that those in Western Europe could render lakes lifeless in Scandinavia. We did not anticipate that the combined impact of fossil-fuel burning here and elsewhere, along with massive destruction of tropical rain forests (as of 1990, 40 million acres a year), could cause a buildup of infrared absorptive gases in the atmosphere, thus affecting global climate, rainfall and even the levels of the oceans.

From the vantage point of 1970, we also had much to learn about the limits of the technologies we counted on to solve our problems. We envisioned new industrial technologies and scientific advances that could provide complete solutions to our problems. Obscure terms, such as *electrostatic precipitators, baghouses,* and *scrubbers* began to appear in the daily press. These devices were to be the cornerstone of efforts to clean up our skies. Filters, holding ponds, aeration lagoons, and bacterial treatment systems were the means we would use to clean up our rivers and lakes. At the same time, in these first years of national commitment industry was expected to invest in pollution controls, to forge ahead as usual but cleanly: clean paper and steel mills, clean power plants and smelters, clean vehicles.

Just a Few Steps Forward

In these last twenty years, U.S. industry and government have spent billions of dollars trying to combat the country's air and water pollution problems. Their reported expenses totaled $85 billion in 1987. (They rose to $100 billion in 1990.) However, it is evident that progress has been limited. Barry Commoner, director of the Center for the Biology of Natural Systems in Queens, New York, analyzed EPA data to identify the actual changes that have occurred in emissions levels of the key pollutants identified in the early seventies (Commoner 1987).

When industrial growth is taken into account, these data indicated discouragingly few areas in which important reductions have occurred. As Commoner discovered, EPA data documented significant reductions of lead emissions (86 percent) since 1970, and related reductions in average lead levels in the blood of Americans (37 percent) between 1976 and 1980. But this success was due to restricting the use of lead in gasoline rather than to the effectiveness of pollution-control equipment to contain and dispose of wastes. Where such equipment was the primary route to environmental protection, the news was less good. EPA data indicated an overall decrease of only 13.2 percent in emissions of the other key air pollutants between 1975 and 1985. Particulates had the best record, having been reduced by 32 percent by 1982, although these emissions increased again by over 4 percent between 1982 and 1985. Sulfur dioxide was reduced by 19 percent from 1975 to 1981, but since then the levels have remained about the same.

Emissions of carbon monoxide—mainly from cars, trucks, and buses—were decreased by 14 percent between 1975 and 1985, but between 1982 and 1985 they again increased. As of 1990 almost 100 urban areas still violated EPA carbon monoxide or ozone standards. Nitrogen oxides emitted by vehicles and power plants presented the most discouraging picture. Between 1975 and 1985, emissions of NO_x actually *increased* by 4 percent. (While SO_x emissions have been reduced, NO_x emissions have increased their contribution to acid rain.)

With respect to U.S. rivers and lakes, Commoner's analysis suggests little or no improvement nationally in the levels of the five standard pollutants that determine water quality: fecal coliform bacteria, dissolved oxygen, nitrates, phosphorous, and suspended sediments. He cited a "recent survey of the trends in American rivers that showed improvement at one-fifth of tested sites but virtually no improvement in water quality at more than four-fifths." Even Lake Erie, the Earth Day symbol of degradation and the subject of major environmental attention, still exceeds federal water quality objectives.

As for chemical pollutants, they have received even less attention. Since 1950 the number of serious chemical pollutants has steadily expanded.

The Enchantment with Progress: Are We Turning a Corner?

The continuing pollution problems that the United States and other industrialized nations confront have been only part of the environmental price we are paying for the progress of the last century. With less than 5 percent of the world's population and 25 percent of the world's annual consumption of resources, U.S. industrial growth and the proliferation of our consumer goods, our energy and transportation systems, and even much of our agricultural activity have rested on the use of fossil fuels, a nonrenewable resource that we are steadily depleting. World fossil-fuel use has increased more than fourfold since 1950. Our enchantment with progress has also rested on the implicit assumption that there would always be somewhere to put our wastes.

While global warming, acid rain, and deforestation are broad issues with long-term implications for life on the planet, the issue of waste has perhaps most directly caused Americans to confront the question of their environmental ethic. Waste brings the issue home to our communities, our streets, our own backyards.

In 1970 we did not dream of a day when there might literally be no place to put the wastes our society had created. We had a vast network of landfills into which we routinely poured billions of pounds a year of industrial toxic and hazardous effluents. Seventy-three percent of municipal solid wastes are still placed on land or injected into deep wells. Thirty-four percent of hazardous chemical wastes are also being placed on land or injected into deep wells.

INFORM's research into chemical and municipal waste problems in the United States over the last seven years has provided important evidence of how painfully slow the pace of actual change has been in the face of the enormous momentum of industrial activity and continuing consumer fascination with new, exciting, colorful, and increasingly disposable products. Our research has also found, however, some signs of recognition based on the experience of the last twenty years that new directions—more radical forms of change—will be needed if we are to achieve a sustainable way of living.

The Issue of Chemical Wastes

During the last two decades of evolving environmental consciousness and the two decades before that, one of the most rapidly expanding sectors of the world economy has been the organic chemical industry. Since it was spawned in the 1940s, this fossil-fuel–based industry's production of chemicals has reached a level of over 220 billion pounds a year in the United States. The industry today produces more than 70,000 commercial chemicals used in making a wide range of consumer and industrial products that have become central to our lives: plastics, solvents, adhesives, paints, pesticides, dyes, and a host of pharmaceuticals.

Many of these chemical-based products have come to replace biodegradable products of natural origin. Plastics have been substituted for paper, leather, wood, ceramics, and metals. Detergents have replaced soap; nitrogen fertilizers have supplanted reliance on soils, organic matter, and nitrogen-fixing crops (the natural source of nitrogen); and chemical pesticides, instead of natural predators, have become the mainstay in fighting insects.

Despite the remarkable qualities of many synthetic organic chemical products, the threats of these and their production processes pose serious questions from the point of view of an environmental ethic. According to a 1984 National Research Council study, barely 10 percent of the chemicals created by this expanding industry have been tested to the point where their long-term safety to health or the environment can be affirmed. Nonetheless, this industry has been allowed to introduce into commercial production more than 1,000 new chemicals each year.

Not only do its products pose more difficult disposal problems than do biodegradable or nontoxic ones, but the polluting by-products of production now contribute almost half of all toxic and hazardous wastes generated in the United States. Some 1.7 billion pounds of solid and semiliquid chemical wastes alone went into treatment and disposal facilities in 1988. More than 4.5 billion additional pounds were discharged into waterways, onto land, or into the atmosphere.

The burgeoning chemical industry has certainly been the subject of increasing regulation over the last ten years. It has had to respond to a host of costly requirements under the U.S. Resource Recovery and Conservation Act, the Clean Air Act, the Clean Water Act, the Superfund Law, and other measures. But governmental requirements, until very recently focused only on strategies geared to trap, contain, and treat toxic wastes, have often resulted in their being moved from one part of the environment to another. Landfilled wastes have leached and become water contaminants. Airborne wastes trapped by bag filters and scrubbers have become solid waste sent to landfills.

Conservation leaders and many other Americans, after almost two decades of observing the limited success of efforts aimed at coping with nontoxic industrial wastes through engineered pollution control, are now raising the call for prevention. Initiatives aimed at source reduction and elimination—at *not* creating both pollutants and wastes in the first place—are now being advanced.

INFORM's case studies of the operation of 29 of the more than 1,000 organic chemical plants in the country found significant pollution- and waste-reduction potential in the chemical industry (Sarokin 1987). Our report concluded that by means such as process and product changes, chemical substitutions, or just better plant housekeeping, companies could actually save money while reducing their wastes by 30 percent, 50 percent, or more. This exciting waste-reduction potential was reaffirmed by a broader national study conducted the same year by the Congressional Office of Technology Assessment in Washington. Yet even as of 1990, this potential had only begun to be tapped due to regulators' and business's continuing main focus on trying to solve their problems through the familiar route of engineered pollution control.

However, there are significant signs of change. After two years of congressional debates, the nation's first Pollution Prevention Act was passed in late 1990. It focuses on reducing industrial plant waste at the source. The EPA has created a new Office of Pollution Prevention, and EPA administrator William K. Reilly is strongly advocating this approach. Almost two dozen states in just two years have launched programs focused on prevention. All this activity signals clear acknowledgment that a vital new approach to industry's wastes is needed, that waste generation has gone too far.

A host of grass-roots groups in the United States and Green party groups in Europe most recently have launched broad waste-prevention campaigns to turn consumers away from chemical-based products that contain toxic or hazardous constituents which may pose a threat to users or to the environment when landfilled or incinerated. They are questioning the production and marketing of the great variety of chemical products, many of which not only are hazardous when produced, used, or disposed of, but are designed for one-time use. Why should our dwindling world supply of fossil fuels be squandered in making so many products that pose risks to natural resources and animal and human health, and for which nontoxic and biodegradable substitutes—products appropriate to a sustainable environment—exist?

The chemical industry continues to grow and flourish. But a new dialogue bound to expand its environmental ethic has definitely begun.

Garbage: Are Citizens Doing Any Better?

New questions are being raised about municipal solid wastes as well. The 440,000 tons of municipal wastes produced each day by 250 mil-

lion Americans constitute one of the highest rates of garbage generation per capita in the world, twice that of most European countries
and Japan. Here, it is not only some polluting industry but individual
citizens who are the cause. The cans, bottles, newspapers, old cars
and tires and refrigerators, batteries, paints, and drugs that account
for our luxurious life-style also choke the existing landfills of the
United States. Here is where the environmental ethic comes closest
to home. Of the almost 20,000 landfills in operation in 1976, barely
6,600 remained in 1989. The rest had been closed because they were
full or because they were polluting local air and water.

Faced with an impending landfill crisis, many communities during
the late 1970s launched an urgent search for a technological fix, one
that would seemingly enable them to perpetuate their waste-
producing ways with impunity. A rush to incineration began. As of
the end of 1990, one hundred and twenty-eight large waste-to-energy
plants were in operation, seventy were in planning, and nineteen
were under construction.

But community after community has become fearful of these facilities' emissions of sulfur dioxide, nitrogen oxides, heavy metals, and
acid gases as well as the possibly carcinogenic dioxins and furans.
They and state and federal regulators are now also uneasy about the
ash that these plants produce, which is increasingly regarded as toxic
because of its heavy-metal and dioxin content.

These concerns further shake the faith of an American public already doubting the abilities of government and industry to site
enough landfills for garbage or build enough pollution-control systems to eliminate industrial waste.

Following several years of demands for recycling, the Environmental Protection Agency in 1988 produced a national garbage management plan containing a goal of 25 percent national waste recycling
by 1997. This was a major step forward for a society whose recycling
rate has been 8 percent to 10 percent overall. But it is a modest goal
when compared to the recycling levels—as high as 50 percent—that
have been achieved in Japanese cities. Among those states taking deliberate steps to equal or exceed Japan's commitment to recycling are
New York State, with a goal of 40 percent recycling and 10 percent

source reduction by 1997; New Jersey, with a 60 percent goal by 1995; and Oregon, with a 50 percent and 56 percent goal by the years 2000 and 2006, respectively.

Stepping back and viewing garbage generation from the perspective of an environmental ethic, what is most striking is the continuing pattern of trying to manage—whether by incineration *or* recycling— all the wastes we create, rather than facing the fact that perhaps we should not be making so many wastes. Franklin Associates, in a consulting study for the EPA, affirms the increase per capita waste generation rate each year, and predicts that the per capita rate for the year 2000 will be 10 percent higher than it is today. A full 32 percent of the U.S. waste stream is comprised of packaging, and new disposable items emerge daily—not just plates and cups, but razors, cameras, printing ribbons, and appliances. Almost 2 percent of the waste stream is disposable diapers. How many of these things are we willing to do without? As of 1990, some of the leading consumer companies in the United States and Europe began to observe a new public mood—and are competing for the "green product" vote. But how broad and deep this shift is remains to be seen.

What Do Conservation Leaders Recommend?

The scientific study and educational programs aimed at government, business, and citizen leaders around the world have in just two short decades bred an astonishing level of knowledge of the precarious position that human activities have created for life on our planet and the nature of the specific threats we face.

Environmental laws have proliferated. Conservation groups have burgeoned in the United States, Europe (even Eastern Europe), and around the world. Their campaigns here and elsewhere have had some real successes. Nonetheless, we are watching our industrialized societies still rapidly depleting the fossil-fuel base and producing ever more unmanageable amounts of pollution and waste. We are also watching as the desperate development efforts of emerging countries destroy the forests, wildlife habitats and wildlife, and water and soil resources needed to sustain not only their lives but ultimately our own.

Meanwhile, since 1950 the world's human population has more than doubled, from 2.5 billion to 5.3 billion people. This makes our situation infinitely more precarious and complex.

The lessons of the last twenty years clearly indicate that just tinkering with our industrial establishment, adding a scrubber here or a baghouse or a landfill there, will not get at the basic problems caused by our eagerly sapping the globe's nonrenewable resources for our near-term economic gain. And while we increasingly applaud the concept of "sustainability," the new encouraging prevention-oriented policies and campaigns have yet to visibly turn the tide of consumption. To achieve a sustainable life-style will mean real and far-reaching changes.

Conservation leaders have clearly articulated an imposing variety of such changes in the *Blueprint for the Environment* (1988). The changes involve more mass transit systems and reduced use of cars; a transition to energy systems relying on renewable energy supplies; a move to much greater reliance on biodegradable and nontoxic materials; a shift in agricultural practices, with reduced use of pesticides and chemical fertilizers; reintroducing natural pest management and practices to sustain and enrich our soils; and steps toward not just recycling but also significantly reducing our wastes at the source, rather than fostering an expanding plethora of "things."

In observing the developing nations, the key lesson of the last twenty years is that our fate is inextricably linked with their own. To achieve a sustainable life on this planet will mean curbing our zealous appetites for production and consumption as well as making some major investments in helping developing nations find an economically and socially sustainable means of living. If not, they may well sink under the burdens of debt and poverty, taking with them the forests, soils, and animal and plant life that are vital for their own and the planet's future.

It is clear that such major changes in the attitudes and actions of the industrialized world, particularly our own country, would represent quite a revolution. As INFORM's research in the United States has shown, industries under the momentum of production, job creation, and sales don't take lightly to the notion of *not* doing things they have been doing, of *not* producing what they can produce. Likewise, men and women, able to afford a glut of consumer products, haven't taken lightly to the notion of *not* buying and having them. Convenience, near-term gain, and comfort still triumph in day-to-day decisions. The problem now does not seem to be a lack of technologies or scientific information, or of public policy recommendations, or even of increasing public enthusiasm for a "greener" life-style. The problem seems to be one mainly involving an underlying ethic stimulating much more dramatic change.

What Have Ethicists and Theologians Seen?

To reach our environmental ethic, as Albert Schweitzer said in 1915, will require the hardest thing of all for mankind to do: to restrain itself lest the earth be destroyed. Writers, social scientists, and theologians, watching and reporting what they have seen in these last decades, have amply reiterated the dilemma.

Robert Heilbroner, in *An Inquiry into the Human Prospect* (1974), expressed skepticism that we could, with all our human intelligence, make the changes required. He identified the "inescapable need to limit industrial growth as mankind's challenge," but he said it was a challenge that would not be met in time, since the challenge of survival lies too far in the future and the inertial momentum of the present industrial order is still too great.

Theologian Thomas Berry expressed the same concern in a different way: "The energy evoked by the ecological vision has not been sufficient to offset the energy evoked by the industrial vision." "We need," he concluded, "an ecological mystique instead of an industrial one." Discussing the expansion of the damage we are doing to our planet, Berry made an especially useful point: "We are used to sticking to the facts," he wrote, "but the facts suggest the problem is deeper."

We conservation leaders focus on scientific studies, public policies, technologies, and social programs as the primary means of change. Crucial as all these efforts clearly are, Berry and many of his fellow writers see as the only basis for achieving broad and lasting change a basic ethical reorientation. Berry emphasizes the need to redefine many terms in our society. For example, what do we mean by *progress* and *profit*? Should these terms be used for activities that spend our environmental capital? Should we go on accepting as the basis for our legal thinking the notion that all rights relate only to the human species? How do we define *education*? Shouldn't children be brought up to understand and marvel at the geological, hydrological, and biological systems that make up the world of which they are a part, rather than to see them as items to be used?

Building the Dialogue

As conservation leaders grope their way along toward environmental progress and as ethical and theological observers of these efforts likewise try to chart paths toward ethical progress, it is clear that a much more significant dialogue is needed between the two groups. The goal of creating a sustainable world relies on both thought and action. Every local conservation and environmental battle embodies elements of the larger ethical issues confronting us. The writings of ethicists, social scientists, and theologians can be greatly enriched by closer contact with and study of these concrete cases.

Likewise, conservation leaders—local, regional, national, or international—can bring into their on-the-ground campaigns elements of an ethical argument that can broaden the terrain on which they are fighting.

Finding time and space for dialogue that can immediately and directly increase the effectiveness of the practitioners and the thinkers is essential if we hope to affect the tens of thousands of everyday actions in the industrialized and developing worlds, whose cumulative effect will meant the survival or the end of the rich and varied life on this planet as we know and treasure it today.

References

BOOKS

Berry, Thomas. 1988. *The Dream of Earth*. San Francisco, Calif.: Sierra Club Books.

Brown, Lester R., et al. 1987. *State of the World* (A Worldwatch Institute Report). New York: W. W. Norton.

Buch, Bruce C., and Larry L. Rasmussen. 1978. *The Predicament of the Prosperous*. Philadelphia: The Westminster Press.

Carson, Rachel. 1962. *Silent Spring*. New York: Houghton Mifflin.

Congressional Office of Technology Assessment. 1986. *Real Source Reduction*. Washington, D.C.: OTA.

Ehrlich, Paul R. and Anne H. Ehrlich. 1981. *Extinction: The Causes and Consequences of the Disappearance of Species*. New York: Random House.

Herschkowitz, Allen, Maarten deKadt, and Joanna Underwood. 1987. *Garbage: Practices, Problems, and Remedies*. New York: INFORM.

Herschkowitz, Allen, and Eugene Salerni. 1987. *Garbage Management in Japan*. 1987. New York: INFORM.

Nash, Roderick Frazier. 1989. *The Rights of Nature*. Madison, Wis.: The University of Wisconsin Press.

Roszak, Theodore. 1972. *Where the Wasteland Ends*. New York: Doubleday.

Sarokin, David, et al. 1987. *Cutting Chemical Wastes*. New York: INFORM.

OTHER PUBLICATIONS

"Blueprint for the Environment," advice to the president-elect from America's environmental community, Washington, D.C. 1988.

"The Bottom Line," an essay by Thomas Berry, Director, Riverdale Center for Religious Research, Riverdale, New York. 1988.

"The Egg," a journal of eco-justice (volume 7, no. 1), Ithaca, N.Y. William Gibson. 1987.

"The Environment," Barry Commoner, *New Yorker Magazine,* June 15, 1987.

"Sermon," Cathedral of St. John the Divine, Joanna D. Underwood, 1988.

"What on Earth Are We Doing?" *Time,* Jan. 2, 1989.

"The Viable Human," an essay by Thomas Berry, Director, Riverdale Center for Religious Research, Riverdale, New York. 1988.

4 Diversification, Minorities, and the Mainstream Environmental Movement

CHARLES JORDAN
Superintendent, Bureau of Parks, City of Portland, Oregon

DONALD SNOW
Project Director and Editor, Conservation Leadership Project

MOST CONSERVATION LEADERS across the United States readily admit that their organizations hold little appeal to people of color. Membership surveys show that national conservation and environmental groups are overwhelmingly white in their makeup. There is no reason to believe that regional, state, or local groups tend to be much different. These facts trouble many conservation leaders. Writing in a 1987 edition of *Audubon Magazine,* National Audubon Society president Peter A. A. Berle decried the scarcity of nonwhite members among his own and sister organizations: "Not one major environmental or conservation organization can boast of significant Black, Hispanic or Native American membership."[1] When the Conservation Leadership Project queried the professional staff and volunteer leaders of over 500 conservation and environmental groups nationwide, the leaders expressed similar dismay. Ninety-five percent of them agreed with the following statement: "Many, perhaps most, minority and poor rural Americans see little in the conservation message that speaks to them." Follow-up interviews with thirty of these leaders revealed the depth of concern that lies beneath that statement: Most leaders surveyed feel that the lack of racial and cultural diversity in their own organizations and throughout the environmental movement makes the movement less powerful and less effective in accomplishing its goals. Some leaders we surveyed said that the lack of diversity is morally wrong—an embarrassment and a smear on their record of public service. In the view of others, it carries strategic liabilities that work against the best interests of diversified grass-roots community groups, who are deprived of the technical, political, and financial benefits that they might enjoy through association with well-established environmental organizations.

While it is difficult to find conservation-environmental groups with policies openly excluding the membership or participation of people of color, the mainstream environmental movement continues to be what historian Stephen Fox calls a "WASP preserve."[2] To the extent that environmentalism is aligned with the liberal, social-change wing of contemporary political debate and action, the movement finds itself nearly alone in its failure to address the key questions of racial and ethnic diversification.

This failure has not gone unnoticed by minority leaders. In January 1990 a group of leaders from various civil rights organizations around the country wrote a letter to the heads of eight national environmental organizations charging them with racism in their hiring practices.[3] So compelling was the substance of their accusations that the New York Times ran an article on this long-simmering dispute between environmentalists and civil rights leaders. While the letter fell short of accusing the organizations of outright refusals to hire or promote on the basis of race, it did complain that the national environmental movement is isolated from the principal victims of pollution—poor and minority communities across the country. The civil rights leaders called for new efforts to diversify staff among these leading environmental groups; specifically, they called for changes in hiring and recruitment to ensure that 30 percent to 40 percent of the environmentalists' staffs are minority persons.

Interestingly, the environmental leaders reacted to the substance of the accusations with partial agreement, though they fell short of endorsing the hiring quotas. National Wildlife Federation president Jay Hair decried the "whiteness of the green movement" and declared that no one is more aware of the problem than environmental leaders themselves. J. Michael McCloskey, chairman of the Sierra Club, admitted that at the time the article appeared, his organization had no blacks or Asian Americans and but 1 Hispanic staffer among its 250 workers. Audubon had only 3 blacks among 350 staffers. The environmental leaders who responded, however, were loath to accept the charge that racism lies at the root of their failures to diversify staff. Several took pains to point out that even earnest efforts at minority recruitment in the past have typically fielded few applicants qualified as environmental professionals and even fewer who will work for the comparatively low wages paid by cause-oriented nonprofits. The problem, these leaders contend, is not so much racism as it is a lack of "fit" between the needs of mainstream environmental-conservation groups and the preparedness of minority citizens to join the staffs of these groups.

But even this dispute over minority hiring, significant though it is, masks a much larger issue. Without meaning to and despite their many efforts to the contrary, environmental advocates have managed to create a kind of exclusive "club of conservation." While the club seems to be open to everyone, and indeed its leaders spend millions on efforts to recruit new members, in actuality the club remains oddly closed to some potential constituents. While the conservation club seems diverse, capable of representing virtually all possible environmental issues, in reality there are certain issues that remain off-limits—they are too disturbing to the carefully constructed strategic plans of the club's leadership. While the club seems to be the best possible blend of grass-roots initiative and technical expertise—of volunteerism and professionalism—in reality the technicians clearly dominate; in most of the club's organizations, the grass roots, represented by the dues-paying membership, has but one role: to support the technical leadership with dollars and the sheer numbers that represent the political clout needed by the professionals as they go about the tasks of effective advocacy.

These conditions exist in the national environmental movement through no conspiracy, no conscious decisions to create policies of exclusion, no malice. They are the natural and expected outcomes of an odd, century-old branch of social policy—natural resource and environmental policy—which has consistently demanded, from as far back as its origins in the Progressive Era, technical competence above all else on the part of its devotees. The so-called mainstream environmental organizations are exclusive because the policy arena in which they operate virtually demands that they must be. The risk they run is that in creating and maintaining the technical expertise they need in order to participate effectively in policy-making, they will find themselves increasingly distanced from their own memberships and increasingly isolated from the grass-roots citizens who feel unwelcome in the club of conservation. They will remain vulnerable to charges of elitism unless and until they develop strategies to maintain more effective contact not only with their own members, but also with the truly grass-roots groups that are working on identical issues.

The most obvious and prominent constituencies that have been inadvertently barred from the conservation mainstream are racial minorities. With few exceptions, Hispanics, Asian Americans, blacks, and Native Americans do not belong to mainstream conservation-environmental groups, are not hired onto their professional staffs, and until very recently were not asked to serve on their boards of directors. While it is true that efforts to hire more minority professionals would help bring greater equity into the environmental movement and would serve to break down the color barrier that separates white environmentalists from nonwhite citizens and organizations, hiring alone will not solve the larger problem of mainstream environmentalists' increasing isolation from the American grass roots. Nor will such hiring ensure that successful environmental-conservation groups, with their undisputed power to influence policy, will necessarily serve minority communities much better than they are serving them now, or make themselves more appealing to the needs and interests of nonwhite citizens. The roots of the problem go much deeper. Unfortunately, many attempts to explain this phenomenon have served merely to reinforce old, inaccurate stereotypes of minorities' needs, interests, and capabilities.

For at least two decades, a handful of sociologists, political scientists, and other commentators have tried to expose the roots of minorities', most particularly blacks', "lack of involvement" in environmental issues and organizations. While a few commentators have suggested that conservation and environmental organizations unintentionally discourage the involvement of people of color, most have approached the question by examining the social and cultural conditions of minority communities that seem to discourage involvement in both environmental issues and environmental organizations. Instead of looking for ways in which the mainstream environmental movement has failed these communities, the bulk of commentary in effect blames the victims. Blacks, Hispanics, Native Americans, and Asian Americans are scrutinized for the reasons why they are not involved in the mainstream of American environmentalism. Understandably, many of these commentaries are repugnant to minority citizens. We will review them later in this chapter.

Discussions revealing why people of color and others are not involved in environmental groups usually focus on the cultural, class, and economic factors that create barriers to involvement, but there are other factors, too, which seem to be poorly understood or remain unrecognized by those who have tried to investigate this phenomenon. The history of the conservation-environmental movement, coupled with the fundamental philosophy of most mainstream environmental groups, offers important clues to the lack of involvement by nonwhite constituencies.

The Racist Legacy of American Conservation

To a very large degree, the enduring whiteness of the green movement is merely a legacy of the movement's own history, dating back to its earliest days. As historian Samuel Hays points out, two of the original, dominant conservation issues—water development and sustained-yield forestry—were largely staged in the American West at a time when ranching and logging were the nearly exclusive domain of white settlers.[4] The kinds of issues raised and the regional settings in which they evolved often were not conducive to the involvement of minorities, even if the racism of the era had not been so pronounced. Still, in the evolution of some early conservation imperatives—fish and wildlife management for one—racism pure and simple foreclosed the involvement of minorities. As Stephen Fox has observed, it was unthinkable that people of color would be granted access to the fishing and hunting clubs that constituted the early wildlife preservation movement.[5] The clubs existed in part as a refuge for well-off Euro-Americans. On sporting adventures among their peers, they could literally leave behind the trials of doing business in the urban melting pot. They could experience the joys of "primitive" fraternity among their racial and ethnic kin.

Even the establishment of nature preserves proved ultimately to carry racist prohibitions. In many areas, people of color were banned from visiting parks and public beaches; in the American West, national parklands that had recently been the domain of Native Americans were suddenly off-limits to their former inhabitants—though not as a matter of outright policy. Indian people simply did not feel welcome in national parks like Glacier in Montana, even though their reservations sometimes bordered the supposedly public pleasuring grounds.[6] Conservationists who had been instrumental in the establishment of these "public" preserves usually did nothing to prevent the exclusion of minority citizens. Clearly, the early conservationists and their organizations behaved in ways that mirrored national attitudes toward blacks, Native Americans, and other minorities.

Even the fledgling Sierra Club, perhaps the most socially progressive of all of the early conservation groups, stumbled when it came to issues of race. Several of its southern California chapters deliberately excluded blacks, Jews, and other minorities from their memberships through a policy of "sponsorship": Established members made sure not to admit anyone who was not Christian and not white. Deploring these practices, the San Francisco chapter, led by David Brower, tried as late as 1959 to introduce a policy favoring inclusion of the "four recognized colors" through the club, but the resolution failed.[7]

Not just color but nationality also sparked exclusionary practices among the Progressive Era and later conservationists. As Fox points out, "the amateur tradition [which characterized early organizing efforts of the conservation movement] inherently drew from a privileged class," namely, successful white Anglo-Saxon Protestants who had come to fear the customs of new immigrants from southern and eastern Europe. The early conservationists, working earnestly to enact creel and bag limits for the taking of wildlife, often believed that Italians, Greeks, and other immigrant groups were responsible for depleting wildlife populations through old-world hunting customs.

Fox explains these Progressive Era attitudes as nothing unique to conservationists: "Racist by modern standards, their attitudes cannot be separated from historical factors specific to the period: the new immigration, the tensions of modernization and rampant progress, cancerous urbanization complemented by the end of the frontier, and the bunker mentality among the old, displaced patricians. Progressive-era conservationists expressed nativist ideas more as prisoners of their time than as conservationists."[8]

And conservationists, Fox attests, continued to mirror national attitudes about race and nationality throughout most of the twentieth century. "Later," he writes, "as the middle class opened to more diverse groups, so did conservation."[9] Still, the movement did not rush to embrace the principles of social diversity in nearly the degree that it came to embrace biological diversity. With the exception of The Wilderness Society, which elevated two Jews, Robert Marshall and Bernard Frank, to positions of national leadership, virtually all of the organizations perpetuated a "WASP hegemony."

Following the Second World War, racism and nativism, while not disappearing from American conservation, were submerged into long-enduring institutional practices. This condition has strangely persisted despite the changes created by the civil rights movement, the decade of the Great Society, and the continued liberalization of American culture with respect to race and creed.

Indeed, during the 1960s and 1970s some environmentalists drew the wrath of civil rights leaders by suggesting that the federal budget (not to mention the congressional attention span) was not great enough to afford environmental protection and minority housing at the same time. The mandate to focus on environmental issues became so severe that many environmentalists seemed to see any other cause, no matter how worthy on its own merits, as a virtual attack on the supreme issues of the environment. In a 1973 poll of its membership, the Sierra Club found its members voting three to one against a proposal to increase the club's involvement with minorities and the urban poor.[10] Such attitudes do not endear environmentalists to their would-be allies in minority communities.

Today it would be difficult indeed to find environmental leaders who are openly racist. The leaders we surveyed are genuinely concerned with the lack of diversity in their organizations and throughout the mainstream movement, yet few can offer ready solutions. The kind of racism their organizations exhibit is institutional: It is deeply woven into the culture of conservation and environmentalism—embedded in and reinforced by old patterns of choice and behavior that have existed in the conservation movement from the beginning and have been carried over into the rise of environmentalism. The proof lies in the enduring whiteness of a movement that otherwise shares much in common with other socially progressive causes.

As many environmental leaders proudly attest, their movement arose with the civil rights and antiwar movements in the middle to late 1960s and shared many common concerns. At the original Earth Day gatherings on April 22, 1970, organizers in many cities were careful to include speakers from civil rights organizations, labor unions, and other progressive causes; and many of the inaugural Earth Day addresses offered by the rising environmental leaders echoed with messages about the interplay of racism, poverty, social injustice, and environmental degradation. Yet soon after the bright green banners of Earth Day had been taken down, the white activists who had put the whole event together from coast to coast seemed to disperse quickly into organizations that then did little to develop thought and action around the interlinks joining poverty and racism with environmental harm. Having heard from the communities of social justice, the white leaders of the budding environmental movement still re-created and perpetuated the same inadvertent, unspoken policies of exclusion that characterized their conservationist forerunners. Today national environmental leaders are faced with embarrassing charges of racism—charges with which they partially acquiesce.

Without question, most conservation and environmental organizations are now fully isolated from historically disadvantaged communities. But just as certainly, the majority of mainstream conservation and environmental leaders, in every region of the country, are aware of this problem and appear committed to rectifying it. What will be the central challenges they face as they move to do so?

The first and perhaps most difficult hurdle they will face is certainly the long-standing, widespread belief that minority citizens are not interested in environmental issues. Among many conservation leaders, comfortably claiming that they have tried but cannot find minorities to hire, this response is virtually reflexive. And no wonder. It is supported, even seemingly justified, by a body of academic and popular literature that tries to account for the supposed lack of minority involvement in environmental issues by offering sociological—even mythological—explanations. Interestingly, most of these explanations are based on the private theories of their authors, not on empirical research. Moreover, many of the theories advanced to account for the noticeable absence of minorities in mainstream environmental-conservation groups grossly misrepresent the scope of environmental activism throughout the twentieth century. Notice in the following summary how often the theories are based on assumptions about conservation and environmental issues that are no more factually based than the assumptions made about historically disadvantaged and minority citizens.

Theories on Minority Involvement

Theories on the environmental involvement of people of color generally fall into two categories. First, a lack of concern (or a gap between concern and action) translates into a lack of involvement. Second, even where concern exists, blacks and other minorities lack the "social qualifications" that accompany participation in the mainstream environmental movement; thus minority action in environmental issues tends to be inchoate.

A lack of concern over conservation issues, coupled with a lack of apprecia-

tion for "white" political strategies, bars minority involvement. These theories tend to suggest that a variety of cultural and historical factors leave blacks and other minorities relatively unconcerned with, or even hostile toward, environmental issues (at least as those issues are developed by mainstream environment organizations). Minority involvement in traditional environmental NGOs, as well as in government agencies charged with environmental management or protection, is thus understandably negligible. The postulated lack of concern might result from one or more of several factors (these are summarized from the existing literature, with modification, from Taylor 1989):[11]

1. Until their basic needs for survival are met and can be reasonably assured for themselves and their children, minority persons will not attempt to satisfy the "aesthetic needs" addressed by mainstream conservation and environmentalism.

2. Education and place of residence (or upbringing) are key indicators of involvement in environmental causes. Since most minority persons have lacked the opportunity to achieve high-level education and are not as likely to live in "pleasant surroundings worth defending," they will be far less likely to be concerned with environmental issues and organizations.

3. Blacks and Native Americans in particular lack the cultural myths that undergird modern environmentalism. Unlike Euro-Americans, Africans and Native Americans did not traditionally view nature as a refuge from civilization; rather, humans and nature were seen as integral to one another, with no emphasis on a dichotomy between natural and human values. These mythological differences contribute to the scarcity of blacks and Native Americans in mainstream environmental groups, which are uniformly founded on the mythic dichotomy between nature and civilization.

4. Postslavery practices in many states and regions banned blacks from parks, beaches, and natural areas. To the extent that conservationist philosophy is engendered through exposure to nature preserves of various kinds, several generations of black

Americans lack the conservation ethic because they were pro-
hibited from developing it through direct encounters with nature.

5. Given the limited range of occupations that blacks were allowed
to pursue in postslavery America, their recreational interests
were generally less outdoors-oriented than those of white society. Blacks who worked under conditions of hard labor out-of-
doors were unlikely to pursue outdoor recreational activities;
hence, they are less likely to advocate natural areas or the range
of environmental issues related to enjoyment of the outdoors.

6. The experience of slavery caused blacks to "hate the land." Land
was not to be valued, sought after, or protected, but despised as
the staging ground for oppression. To the extent that conservation and environmentalism are tied to a reverence for land and
a desire to acquire, protect, or manage land, many blacks are
excluded because of their negative associations with land. (A
counterargument suggests that not land hatred but land hunger
characterizes black attitudes toward land: Deprived of ownership, many blacks came to see land as a place of refuge and independence. Participation in conservation, however, puts one
at some distance from land, especially insofar as conservationists favor public ownership and management of scenic and biologically significant land; thus, conservation strategies historically were less involved with outright ownership and personal
use of land and may be viewed as impediments to personal
ownership.)

7. Environmentalism is often characterized by the effective use of
personal, individual contact with decision makers (generally a
white political strategy) rather than mass action (more likely a
nonwhite political strategy). In addition, environmental advocacy seems to demand a technical-bureaucratic approach, and
to the extent that it does, it remains unappealing to blacks and
other minorities as a form of political action.[12]

In several of these theories, conservation and environmentalism are
viewed as being based on exclusively aesthetic concerns—presum-

ably the preservation of scenic beauty, or animals and habitats that are not "useful" as much as they are "appealing." Other theories reduce the national environmental enterprise to considerations of land preservation, especially the preservation of wildlands. Questions of human health and survival, questions pertaining to the protection of nonscenic natural systems against pollution and other forms of contamination, questions of economic and natural resource sustainability are simply dropped from the conservationist equation. Moreover, several of these theories are founded on and reinforce a long-standing belief that conservationists come primarily from the wealthy class: For the most part, they are patricians and upper-middle-class professionals whose conservation "hobby" focuses on defending their own neighborhoods (presumably exurban estates or very nicely designed suburban communities) from unseemly encroachments. Once again, the issues they take on, in this view, are primarily aesthetic, and are thus of little interest to people struggling to raise their own standard of living.

Clearly, those who hold these views ignore many of the primary battles that conservationists and environmentalists have led throughout this century—battles that reach far beyond aesthetic questions. Air and water quality, open government and the democratic process, habitat protection, carrying capacity and biogeography, waste disposal, mined-land reclamation, energy planning, coastal zone and waterways protection, sustainable forestry and agriculture, sustainable economics and other issues related to renewable resources are a few of the primary environmental issues that are ignored in several of these theories.

Moreover, at least two of the theories (3 and 7) depend on the acceptance of stereotypes of traditions and preferences among various minority groups. The contention that blacks and other minorities are somehow disposed to *prefer* strategies of political mass action over a technical approach (to issues that are, plain to see, often highly technical in nature) is offensive to many. Said one Hispanic leader: "With respect to third-world people within the U.S. . . . being more prone toward the street marches than the technical approach—my God, if we had the kind of budget the National Wildlife Federation has, we, too, would hire technicians, engineers, and scientists instead of marching on the streets and having to replace our shoes every few months."

As to the contention that black and Native American tribal traditions are not based on the Cartesian dichotomy between humans and nature, and therefore forestall the involvement of these people in conservation issues, this seems to be a case of overstretching a theory to the breaking point. It is true that some Native American and Native Alaskan leaders object to the philosophical duality inherent in, for example, wilderness preservation, and thus refuse to participate in efforts to place certain lands in the federal wilderness system. But to suggest that these same people and groups would then refuse to participate in any or all other environmental issues—pollution control, for example—seems to stretch the case to incredulity. The concomitant belief that tribalism in African nations would dominate the conservationist sentiments of American blacks several generations removed seems an even longer stretch of theory.

Environmental concern exists but societal constraints bar minorities from mainstream involvement. This second set of theories tends to be less farfetched, for these are based on empirical observations of the social prerequisites that accompany membership in volunteer organizations. These are intended, for the most part, to explain why the "action gap" exists—that is, why minority persons do not translate their environmental concern into active membership in mainstream conservation–environmental groups:

1. Many well-established environmental or conservation organizations have their historical roots in issues related to environmental recreation—outdoor activities emphasizing hiking, climbing, wildlife watching, sport hunting and fishing, and so forth. While many such organizations have evolved to create even greater emphases on issues unrelated to environmental recreation, minority persons will be less involved in them because they often lack the unspoken social prerequisites that usually

accompany organizational membership. The environmental recreational experiences of many minority groups and persons have been constrained by social policy, tacit or overt, and by life circumstances.[13] They will tend to feel that they do not qualify for membership, no matter how great their concern for the issues pursued by such organizations. While virtually no conservation-environmental group deliberately excludes people who lack these experiences, they do tend to attract primarily the ones who belong to the "club" of outdoors enthusiasts. Others, especially people of color, may not feel welcome in these organizations.

2. Environmental action and the kind of education that normally precedes it go hand in hand. Without the cultural and societal incentives leading to careers (or volunteer activism) in the environment, minority children do not choose them. This explains the scarcity of minority persons in the fields of environmental management and regulation, forestry and public lands management, and other environmentally related careers in government, private enterprise, and activist organizations. The educational inducements that seem to preface conservation vocations and avocations will continue to be lacking until the right societal incentives are created and nurtured. As environmental issues become more visible in minority communities, professional and volunteer engagement in these issues will grow.

3. Environmental advocacy often seems to imply an attack on economic and job-creating activities. For communities struggling with extremely high levels of unemployment (with some Indian reservations having the highest unemployment of any communities in the country), environmental quality is often portrayed as an unacceptable trade-off against jobs. Among the historically disadvantaged, the onerous effects of this trade-off are especially acute. Even where environmental concern runs high among minority groups, the implications of the trade-off often thwart environmental action or render minority persons hostile toward it.

The Invisibility of Minority Environmentalism

These latter theories, while speaking more sensitively to the societal and economic constraints that bar minority entry into mainstream environmental organizations, still tend to obscure a very important point: People of color are, in fact, deeply involved in environmental issues and have been for some time. Nor do they adequately account for minorities' legitimate interest in environmental issues. The truth is minority involvement in these issues is today diverse, widespread, effective and, most significantly, growing at a very rapid rate. The fact that this involvement remains somehow invisible to many in the environmental mainstream, as well as in the national media, is not the fault of the many minority persons who have stepped beyond the barriers to perform effective environmental advocacy. Their lack of participation in mainstream organizations should not be construed in any sense to indicate a lack of interest or involvement in environmental issues.

A few scholars and commentators in the popular press have recently begun demolishing facile preconceptions about minority environmental action, which goes largely unreported by the mainstream media in exactly the same way that many other issues and initiatives pursued by nonwhite Americans go unreported. Minority environmental involvement is growing at a very rapid pace and is part of a new grass-roots environmental movement nationwide that does not adhere to the conventions of the so-called mainstream conservation-environmental organizations, and indeed is comprised precisely of the individuals and communities who often feel left out of the mainstreamers' organizations. Minority environmentalists continue to create their own outlets for expression of environmental concern and action quite outside of the environmental mainstream. The fact that much of this labor remains invisible to the national media and to many people in the mainstream environmental movement is a point that is not lost on the "new environmentalists."

The conventional definition of the environmental movement is partially to blame for the invisibility of minority environmental advocacy in the United States. Many minority organizations that were founded on an agenda of civil rights, social justice, and broad issues of economic equity are turning increasingly to environmental issues as well, but lack the familiar tags of environmentalism and thus remain invisible to the rest of the movement. Exacerbating the invisibility is the fact that minority environmental programs, regardless of their institutional location, are fairly new. Official revelations that minority communities suffer disproportionately greater effects from pollution are largely phenomena of the 1980s; much of the organizing that occurred around these findings has been in the affected communities. The time to pay attention to these significant improvements is overdue.

Rewatering the Grass Roots—The "New Environmentalism"

Writing in a 1988 edition of *The Progressive,* scholars Robert Gottlieb and Helen Ingram offer what is perhaps the clearest definition of the "new environmentalism."[14] They observe that while the budding environmental movement of the 1970s fashioned and promoted a legislative agenda of key environmental issues (clean air and water, endangered species protection, and Superfund, to name three), movement leaders and organizations spent most of the 1980s in an attitude of retrenchment—essentially in a defensive posture—while making their organizations substantially more "professionalized." In a manner resembling their conservationist forebears, the well-established environmentalists of the eighties began to believe that greater expertise, not greater political power, was needed to manage egregious environmental problems. What began as a newly revitalized grass-roots movement following Earth Day scored a host of astonishing legislative victories, then quickly took on the tone and manner of a legal-technical elite. According to Gottlieb and Ingram, the "mainstream environmentalists relied heavily on lobbying, litigation and 'science' to achieve their objectives, creating in the process a kind of cult of expertise."[15] But the grass roots would not be stamped out:

At the same time [that the mainstream environmentalists continue to "bureaucratize" their organizations] . . . something different has begun to make itself felt—a movement, or rather a number of movements, focusing on issues affecting their communities and the quality of their lives. These tend to be neighborhood or community efforts whose principal concern is the urban and industrial environment, though they are not indifferent to the state of the natural environment as well. . . . The arena for these organizations tends to be the community, and their issues center on local democratic control rather than on national, bureaucratic resolutions.[16]

Gottlieb and Ingram write that instead of embracing these new organizations—most of them comprised entirely of volunteers with no professional staff—some leaders of the mainstream environmental NGOs regard them as anything but allies:

[S]ome environmental leaders now regard grass-roots movements as potential threats to their new-found respectability as reasonable negotiators. As heirs to their conservationist forerunners' deference to expertise, establishment environmentalists are embarrassed by the lack of scientific sophistication in the grass-roots movements.

What is most striking about the grass-roots efforts, however, is their democratic thrust, similar in some ways to the student, civil-rights, and women's movements that flourished a generation ago. Instead of embracing expertise, they have developed self-taught experts. Instead of concentrating on lobbying and legislation, they have resorted to popular action and citizens' lawsuits. They have become organizations of active members rather than rosters of dues-payers on mailing lists.[17]

Most of these new grass-roots groups trace their origins to neighborhood struggles against hazardous waste facilities and other industrial installations that threaten to pollute local environs. Depending on the region of the country, many of these new groups are multiracial and many, perhaps the majority, are led by women and people of color—two groups noticeably absent from the leadership of the mainstream NGOs. The new environmentalism practiced by these groups proves that the issue of environment is as accessible and important to people of color as any other issue affecting their lives; it gives the lie to the notion that they are not interested in, or are even hostile to, the kinds of issues championed by mainstream conservationists and environmentalists—namely, air and water quality, the effects of pollutants on humans and other life-forms, broad issues of land use, and the decision-making process that affects all of these.

Some will argue that there is nothing at all new about these organizations—that they are simply the most recent incarnation of local environmental activism. But that view is incorrect. There are scores of local, state, and regional conservation-environmental organizations all over the country that more closely resemble the establishment environmental organizations at the national level in makeup and orientation toward issues. It is not merely that the new environmentalists are local that distinguishes them; it is their composition and manner of operation. The differences between the mainstreamers and the new environmentalists can be summarized in part as differences in organizational culture. While the mainstreamers tend to rely on hierarchical models of organization, the new environmentalists are more highly democratized. The former tend to see themselves as environmental professionals working to influence the established order of environmental management by working within the system. The latter tend to doubt whether the system, as it is currently constituted, will ever work for them; as often as not, they distrust "professionals" in the environmental field, regardless of whether the professionals come in governmental, business, or NGO packaging.

Another essential difference between the new grass-roots environmentalists and their establishment counterparts is a matter of organizational emphasis and direction: While the traditional groups have amassed memberships to underwrite staff experts in law, science, and policy, the grass-roots groups are comprised of members who are personally involved in the issues (but usually lack technical expertise). In the manner in which they establish their base of support and the ways in which they select issues and strategies, the grass-roots groups are essentially *political,* while many of their establishment counterparts have become essentially *technical.*[18]

Indeed, a major complaint that the new environmentalists voice about their mainstream cousins relates to the perception that the environmental establishment scrupulously avoids political solutions to environmental problems in its rush to participate in "technical fixes." Lois Gibbs, a leading critic of mainstream environmental organizations, said this:

> Environmentalism's history shows that we succeed when we consciously and systematically focus on building a political base of support within the American public. This holds true for *all* environmental issues, whether they be national parks, endangered species, toxic waste, or garbage. Efforts to preserve and improve the environment are sure to be set back, if not fail outright, when advocates for the environment forget or ignore the fact that environmental causes are just as political as any other public policy issue.[19]

The kind of politics contemplated by Gibbs is not the power-brokering politics of lobbying on Capitol Hill, but the street-level organizing of grass-roots citizens who feel that their government fails to protect them from various forms of environmental harm. Gibbs says that the new environmentalism, probably the fastest-growing segment of the national environmental movement, is so appealing to the grass roots precisely because its leaders merge environmental issues with issues of social justice. Gibbs calls the result "environmental justice" and claims that it serves to place environmental issues alongside fundamental questions of fairness and equity. And therein also lies the reason why so many well-established mainstreamers will not rush to embrace the new environmentalism: The mainstreamers, by and large, are uncomfortable with the agenda—indeed, the very vocabulary—of social justice. They rarely use the language of political and economic empowerment. Indeed, the very word *empowerment* tends to be absent from their vocabulary. Some even recoil at the suggestion that they are *activists,* apparently believing that the political connotations of the word somehow weaken their credibility as practical, scientifically based negotiators. As Gottlieb and Ingram write, many of them are indeed embarrassed by the lack of technical sophistication that seems to be inherent in grass-roots movements. Moreover, they have not created organizational systems that lend themselves to the kinds of internal decision making that the new environmentalists favor.

According to new-environmentalist critics of the mainstream movement, decision making as practiced by the conventional NGOs follows a top-down approach, with board members and other leaders setting agendas with little input from the grass roots. Organizational behavior thus mimics the corporate approach to problem solving. As minority citizens and other historically disadvantaged groups are working within their communities in direct response to local threats of pollution, resource exploitation, and land-use decisions over which community groups have little or no control, they quickly learn to focus on the decision-making process as an issue itself—often the primary issue in the dispute. They feel that the way developmental decisions are made virtually guarantees that they and their communities will be excluded. It is thus an easy step to observe that organizations favoring the same kind of approach to internal decision making are also not to be trusted or respected. The top-down approach seems to them to be disempowering, paternalistic, and exclusive, no matter where it is used. When mainstream environmentalists arrive to "help" with community issues, they are thus confronted with a dilemma: The people they intend to help often see them as indistinguishable from "the enemy." The mainstreamers, the regulators, and the developers all seem to use the same language, wear the same clothing, and employ the same kind of decision-making process. They seem all too willing to "cut a deal," leaving the affected communities at risk, uninformed, and disempowered.

Thus, in the policy arena, the mainstream and new environmentalists can *seem* to be working side by side on identical issues, while in reality they are at odds over the most fundamental questions in a democracy: Who shall choose, and how shall the choices be made?

The Lack of Minority Involvement as a Reflection of Organizational Dynamics

These kinds of questions are not mere philosophical quibbles; they go to the very heart of minority involvement—or the lack of it—in mainstream environmental organizations. And there is no small concern over these questions on the part of mainstream environmental leaders. Still moored to their volunteer roots yet increasingly pressed into the technical and managerial aspects of environmental issues, mainstream environmental organizations suffer from a kind of identity crisis over these fundamental questions of empowerment and decision making. Many leaders of successful mainstream groups admit that they are in a quandary over how to involve their members meaningfully in issues of daunting technical complexity. As one leader said: "This is the age-old problem of democracy—the conflict between efficiency and representation." Mainstream leaders are well aware that their memberships in many cases are not participants in the same way, or to the same degree, that members of the grass-roots groups are. But to recapture that kind of membership activism seems to many hardworking environmental leaders to be a kind of organizational regression to a time when amateur activism was most needed—which is to say, a time when political advocacy was the key to getting legislation passed or getting national attention paid to an emerging issue.

It is within the context of that identity crisis that the failure to embrace minority persons and issues is best understood. Yet many critics of the mainstream movement, rushing to excoriate national environmental organizations for their "institutional racism," fail to appreciate that the mainstreamers and their organizations act the way they do largely in response to the nature of the issues they are trying to address, and the long-standing history of natural resource protection and regulation.

National environmental organizations adopted their current emphasis on the technical-scientific aspects of their trade largely as a matter of perceived necessity. Having used the political process so successfully to create new federal and state programs in environmental management, mainstream environmentalists moved on to the next series of tasks: trying to ensure that these programs were enforced and effective. In so doing, they inadvertently replicated their conservationist forerunners' reliance on a technical elite.

At the same time, they were responding to the financial challenges posed by running their hydra-headed, growth-oriented organizations. And again, their choices tended toward the technical: The successful organizations—the survivors—found and hired the experts they needed to mount sophisticated revenue-raising campaigns, often based on the building of substantial organizational memberships through the use of direct mail. They soon discovered that one strategy seemed to feed the other: As their "official" credibility grew through a moderate, technical approach to issues (rather than continuous reliance on confrontational political action), their memberships grew apace. By becoming more mainstream in their approach to the issues, they seemed to be attracting a more mainstream constituency (though not necessarily a very involved one).

Thus, mainstream environmentalists *chose* to concentrate on gathering middle-class, affluent constituents who would write generous checks but not involve themselves on the ramparts. In the process, they gathered memberships that in most cases are overwhelmingly urban-suburban in makeup. In the eyes of the movement's leadership, this union was a natural fit: The mailing lists thus acquired for direct-mail campaigning, for example, work better when culturally and educationally matched with existing members. Thus wedded to direct mail as their principal recruitment tool, the largest environmental organizations found that their memberships virtually self-selected. These organizations began to master the art of recruiting demographically similar members; the dissimilar not only did not join, they usually were not asked.

But more important, the choice to develop an affluent, middle-class membership grew logically from the desire to achieve greater effectiveness at the deepest levels of policy-making. The organizations no longer wanted to attack the environmental management establishment; they wanted to run it. At the very least, they wanted to see their ideas clearly reflected in the lawmaking, regulations, and administrative behavior of government; and that desire prompted them to become increasingly competent in the science, economics, and administration underpinning environmental management.

Accompanying and prodding these organizational tendencies was sheer competition: The explosion in numbers of environmental groups following Earth Day made hard competitors of them all.

Claiming major policy victories led to increased support, as did careful, professional attention paid to the demographics of membership building. Shedding the radical skin of their amateur past seemed necessary to achieve that goal. Part of the unfortunate fallout was the continuing disenfranchisement of constituencies that have never entered the mainstream of American environmentalism.

What were once visceral campaigns on issues proposed by the most vociferous members of organizations' boards became carefully constructed plans to move an issue strategically from beginning to resolution, building the organization through careful outreach and public relations as the issue progressed. As the organizations matured into stable institutions, they tended to fight fewer brush fires, focused their agendas more sharply, and acted far less on the impulses of perceived emergencies. Some of them achieved what one leader described as "laser-beam focus." Coincidentally, many of them began to serve the needs and demands of their members less and the strategic imperatives of their board leaders and staff specialists more.

Those communities that might have been aided by the increasingly powerful, strategically driven environmental movement but were not thus found themselves lost in the cleavage between the twin imperatives of organizational growth and respectable technical effectiveness. The newly empowered mainstreamers, many of whom had their origins in the older conservation movement, fled from the radical amateur tradition as fast as they could while they courted—quite professionally and successfully, it turned out—a new legion of middle-class adherents.

What communities of color quickly learned from the environmental movement, by and large, was that independence from it worked best. The national organizations, even those purporting to offer technical assistance to local groups, proved unreliable to many new community groups tackling environmental issues through more political means. In some instances, established environmental organizations appeared to be on the side of the developers and regulatory agencies—a trinity of "reasonable" authorities that often seemed to agree with each other far more often than they disagreed. The grass-roots communities often felt lost in the arcane shuffle among the experts.

There is perhaps no more telling a setting for the tensions that ensued than the Indian reservations.

The Curious Environmental Legacy of the American Indian

While the early conservationists fought (or neglected) racial integration and sometimes waxed xenophobic, they remained peculiarly fond of American Indians. This fondness continued through most of the twentieth century; it ended only recently (though if one studied only the deep ecology–bioregionalism wing of the environmental movement, one would readily conclude that it has not ended at all but has increased). Indians were extolled by various conservation leaders—John Muir, Gifford Pinchot, George Bird Grinnell, Charles Lindbergh, Stewart Udall, Sigurd Olson, and others—for the legacy they left to their conquerors: clean air and water, full, virgin forests and grasslands, abundant wildlife—all despite what was certainly heavy use by large numbers of native people.[20] Indian conceptions of nature, though not well understood by many conservationists, were often lumped together into a monolithic "Indian view" and praised for their careful consideration of living things, ecological relationships, and future generations. What is odd about the conservationists' fondness—and indeed the environmentalists' uncertainty—about American Indians' use of the continent is that it has almost invariably existed without reference to any particular Indian *persons*. Neatly ensconced on the reservations, Indian peoples did not have to be dealt with directly, in the way one had to deal with rural and urban blacks and the incoming "foreigners." For many, Indian views could wistfully romanticize groups still surviving but unmet.

Contemporary environmentalists are far less certain about the Indian view of nature than their earlier counterparts. For one thing, Native Americans have become more prominent in society: Their reservation lands are studied and sought after for minerals and other uses; their governments exert claims for levels of sovereign authority and use of various resources (water, for example) to a degree that would have astonished non-Indians a generation ago. These original

Americans now must be dealt with, for despite the many problems that beset the reservations, the self-determination of Indian people is on the rise. Through the 1970s and 1980s, Native Americans surely rose into the consciousness of environmentalists, whose romantic views of them were sometimes shattered by the realities.

Environmentalists have trouble reconciling some tribes' interests in large-scale industrial development with environmentalist interests in the deindustrialization (or simple preservation) of rural areas. With unemployment soaring to levels as high as 80 percent on the reservations, federal support plummeting during the Reagan years (James Watt called the reservations "islands of failed socialism"), and few solid economic prospects on the horizon, even the most progressive tribal leaders have sometimes favored the siting of new power plants, mines, and other polluting facilities on their reservations. Meanwhile, other tribes, with the blessing and support of environmentalists, have moved to designate reservation airsheds as Class I, thus giving them the most protective designation possible under federal law. That tribal leaders would not automatically join environmentalists in "the defense of the planet"—according to the environmentalist view of what constituted the defense—was an egregious and astonishing revelation to some. Environmentalists learned that Indian tribes are a varied lot: There is no monolithic Indian view of nature. Nor do Indian views naturally or necessarily conform with environmentalist views. Sometimes they are quite the opposite.

The Sierra Club Legal Defense Fund's coordinating attorney, Vawter Parker, writing in a 1985 edition of *High Country News,* decried the Navajos' willingness to enter into a partnership to build a new power plant on a reservation. His editorial closed with this passage:

Conservationists may themselves have painted too ideal a picture of Indian attitudes toward land, and it is perhaps unfair to expect native religious values to fare any better than those professed by other Americans. Discarding unrealistic expectations and stereotypes, even well-intentioned ones, can ultimately be beneficial. The alliance of the largest Indian tribe with Bechtel, GE and a major utility to build another power plant in the Southwest illustrates almost too well the inadequacy of some old assumptions.[21]

Other environmentalists and nonenvironmental organizations continue to clash with Indians over the issue of treaty rights that give Native Americans special protection for the taking of fish and wildlife both on and off their reservations. The ceremonial use of eagle feathers for Indian religious practices sparked a controversy between several tribes and the National Audubon Society. Some animal rights activists continue to mount an assault on native Alaskan peoples over the killing of fur-bearing animals for sale on the international market; even subsistence hunting practices, which have existed for millennia, are attacked as inhumane by these groups. The native peoples thus vilified are understandably upset over these efforts; just as understandably, some tend to paint all environmental advocates with the same tarry brush.

To be sure, there are many examples of successful coordination of environmentalist and Native American agendas and interests. In several western states, tribal traditionalists and non-Indian environmentalists have joined interests in attacking industrial development that would have needlessly destroyed both environmental and Native American religious resources (protected under the federal American Indian Religious Freedom Act) outside of reservations. Environmentalists have also been supportive of some Indian claims to water in the semiarid and arid West—even when those claims implied future water development. But the misunderstandings persist, partly because of the scarcity of Indian people among the ranks of environmental groups.

The trouble that has occurred between urban environmentalists and rural tribal people is indicative of the clash of cultures and expectations one encounters through contemporary environmentalism. Though the tribes are peculiar among America's minority groups because of their substantial land base (the reservation system) and their unique status under the law, many of the struggles and misunderstandings that they continue to suffer at the hands of the environmental community are indicative of a larger problem: Environmentalists routinely fail to understand or recognize the needs, desires, and cultural differences of people of color, and often rural people as well, whose livelihoods are often based on the use of natural resources. It is very difficult, for example, for many well-off suburban environmentalists to understand or have much compassion for the life circumstances of historically disadvantaged people—especially when those people have so long remained so invisible to the larger society.

Thus, it is little wonder that environmental organizations now stand virtually (if unintentionally) alone in matters of deliberate racial and cultural integration—the last enduring "WASP preserve" within the American social-change movement. How can environmental organizations enrich their involvement with communities and organizations of color? What incentives, partnerships, or inducements are needed in order to bring people of color into the mainstream environmental movement?

The Report of the Minorities Roundtable of the Conservation Leadership Project

In order to offer constructive recommendations for diversifying American conservation-environmental organizations, the Conservation Leadership Project brought together a roundtable of leaders from black, Hispanic, native Alaskan, Native Hawaiian, Native American, and Asian American communities. These leaders met with leaders from several mainstream environmental organizations to consider the issues and strategies of diversification. They were given a paper representing, in part, a review of existing literature on the barriers to minority involvement in the mainstream environmental movement, and asked to focus their comments and concerns partly with respect to what various commentators and scholars have said about the subject. The following is the substance of their report to the Leadership Project.

WHY DIVERSIFY?

The group first asked a very fundamental question: Why diversify? Are there strategic reasons why mainstream environmentalists should deliberately open their organizations to those who currently feel disenfranchised from them? Are there moral and ethical reasons? Is it in the interest of communities of color to enlist in the mainstream environmental movement? The group agreed on the following reasons to diversify:

1. Minority voter blocs are forming convincingly in many regions of the country. In Texas, for example, 51 percent of the electorate will soon be comprised of black and Hispanic voters. All over the country, effective environmental agendas could be formed through coalitions of environmental and minority interests.

2. The voting record of the Black Congressional Caucus is the most solid environmental record in Congress. Clearly, blacks in Congress understand and support environmental issues, despite the fact that so few blacks are involved with the mainstream advocates of these issues. Given the demonstrated sensitivity of black congressional representatives to environmental issues, it makes obvious sense to unite the interests of blacks and environmentalists through organizational channels.

3. The demographic shift toward more women and minorities in the workplace (85 percent by the year 2000) makes diversification both desirable and inevitable.

4. Reacting positively to that demographic shift will demand and increase the sophistication of mainstream environmental organizations. Their current lack of diversification bears evidence of a lack of sophistication.

5. Diversity is ecologically and biologically correct.

6. Diversity is ethically and morally correct.

7. America's greatest asset is its human diversity, its multicultural heritage. Diversity will be required to solve the enormous environmental problems that loom ahead.

8. Diversity broadens the perspective. The broader the perspective, the more likely that solutions to myriad social and environmental problems will be found.

9. The burden of the question should be shifted. The question for

the mainstream environmental groups should be, Why are we not diverse; what are we doing wrong?

The degree of commitment to diversification and the sort of diversification favored by the environmental Group of Ten leaders (the heads of ten of the largest and most influential environmental groups in the country) remain unclear to the roundtable group. Leaders of the Ten and other mainstream organizations seem to favor diversification for various reasons. Some believe it is ethically and morally correct, and have personal commitments to diversification. Others, viewing the political power of minorities, are politically motivated. Still others recognize the implications of the shift in workplace demographics toward minorities and women, and want to be prepared for the future.

Members of the roundtable emphasized that diversification has to be defined so that it serves everyone, not merely the political agendas of the nation's largest environmental groups. Said one roundtable member: "The Group of Ten sees diversification as bringing more numbers on board to do the same job; we see it as a way to concentrate on a new job."

Diversification must apply to membership, leadership, and the agendas of the mainstream groups. The membership and leadership can be diversified through sensitive recruitment; work on the environmentalists' agendas to make them appealing to minorities will be a much more difficult task. The mainstream environmental movement, in order to deliver the right messages to minority people, the rural poor, and other disenfranchised citizens, must reestablish its commitment to equity and social justice. Moreover, the agendas must be open at the highest levels to input from minority persons if such diversification is to occur.

RECOMMENDATIONS FOR CHANGE

The roundtable group created a series of recommendations for diversifying the mainstream environmental movement. *The group felt that diversification implies a broad restructuring of the agendas of most international-national environmental organizations. Ultimately, diversification must relate to the central mission of each organization.* There was a strong sense among the group that many of the international-national organizations exist largely for the purpose of self-perpetuation; in their competitive rush to garner larger check-writing memberships and court wealthy patrons, they have effectively removed themselves from meaningful grass-roots involvement. The question of whom the mainstream environmental movement actually serves is thus an open question. If it wants to serve all of the people and become an active player in the field of social justice, then each organization must carefully examine its mission and its own concept of constituency. "Environmental organizations ought to be working for everyone, not merely for some small, self-selected elite."

Here are the recommendations developed by the roundtable.

Recruitment of Staff. Strong minority representation among the professional staffs of the organizations would do much to help adjust the agendas and improve recruitment of minority members. Recruitment of staff might involve the following:

1. Recruitment through environmental programs at the historically black colleges and universities, and through various minority fellowship programs that already exist (for example, the Minority Urban Fellowship Program administered by Hunter College).
2. Direct support through new fellowship programs for minority students, with provision for "pay-back time," in which the student agrees to work for the sponsoring organizations for a period of time after graduation.
3. New programs designed to forgive student loans for minority students who go to work in the environmental movement.
4. Involvement in the Environmental Consortium for Minority Outreach, funded in part by The Green Group (formerly the Group of Ten) and other national environmental organizations. Working with the EPA, the program is helping to create a new

network of minority environmental professionals. This network can provide a ready pool of minority candidates for professional positions among the conservation–environmental NGOs.

Recruitment of Members.   Mainstream environmental organizations can certainly use their skills at direct mail and other forms of membership recruitment to build minority constituencies, but new messages will have to be developed first. In order to recruit effectively, most organizations will need to show evidence of a serious commitment to serving grass-roots constituencies and expanding their work into the arena of social justice. Once these changes are made, recruitment will be more effective. Here are some ways to recruit:

1. Offer sliding-scale membership fees.
2. Offer useful information to minority communities as part of a canvass.
3. Advertise through popular magazines with large minority readership.
4. Alter the text and graphics of solicitation appeals; use "interpreters" from the target communities to make sure the messages are tailored to fit.
5. Create multilingual environmental education videos with nonwhite "actors."
6. Promote public lands, parks, and other environmental recreational facilities as places open to minority people for recreation, reunions, education programs, and other uses.
7. Roundtable members felt that too many conservation-environmental groups are simply too quiet: They do not effectively and aggressively take their messages into the homes and businesses of the majority of Americans. The recommendation: Alter the "low-profile" approach; make the organizational mission more available and accessible, and invite review and comment from organizational members and others.
8. Roundtable members observed that industry's efforts to blunt the effectiveness of the environmentalist message work very well in some minority communities; "job blackmail" is a tried-

and-true strategy for convincing historically disadvantaged communities and individuals that environmental efforts constitute threats to livelihood. The recommendation then: Develop public affairs departments to compete directly with industry's efforts to "win" constituents.

Improving the Agenda. There is no easy prescription for altering agendas in ways that will appeal to more diverse constituencies, but members of the roundtable felt that such alteration is the key to garnering involvement that is not mere tokenism. Environmental organizations committed to diversity will need to find their own paths to change, and they will need the assistance of minority persons in the topmost levels of the organization. While not prescribing a list of issues per se, the following represents some recommendations for improving organizational agendas in ways that will appeal to people of color:

1. Recognize that social justice and environmental issues are inseparable.
2. Be willing to commit the time and the money it will take to restructure the organizational agenda. Tokenism will serve no one.
3. Assess and face the inevitable conflict between mainstream environmental groups and "Third World minority communities"; commit to protecting everyone, not just the elite.
4. Recognize the ongoing need for grass-roots, social justice organizations in our de facto segregated society, and commit to supporting them.
5. Where possible, assist in efforts at congressional redistricting; file amicus briefs and otherwise assist in the legal work to assure equitable minority representation in Congress.
6. Think through new approaches to offer technical assistance to grass-roots environmental organizations; look for the linkages between the national agenda and the local agenda in any given issue.

How Can Minority Leaders Help? The change prescribed here is a two-way street. While offering constructive recommendations to mainstream environmental organizations, minority communities, groups, and leaders must realize that they also have some work to do, primarily in the field of environmental education:

1. Educate minority citizens, especially children, about the supreme importance of environmental issues.
2. Change minorities' definition of social justice to include environmental justice.
3. Promote environmentalism as a key aspect of economic self-sufficiency on the Indian reservations especially.
4. Recognize the diversity of opinion, issues, and styles among the existing mainstream organizations. Some will be helpful, committed, and receptive; others not. Don't condemn them all because some will not participate.

Given the long history of exclusion, members of the roundtable noted, it is an open question whether minorities can set aside their unfavorable opinions of environmentalists and give new partnerships a chance. There is a strong sentiment among some civil rights and social justice advocates that the national environmental movement, from Earth Day 1970 to the present, has had every opportunity to build organizations that include people of color and advocate issues of interest to them, and has failed. The question now remains: "How do we know they're sincere this time?" Clearly, evidence of the will to change must emerge from the mainstream environmental movement itself. One risk it runs by not accepting this challenge is to see minority communities of all kinds gradually grow their own environmental movement, quite separate from—and often in opposition to—the mainstream movement.

Now is a propitious moment for minority and mainstream environmentalists to come together. Perhaps for the first time, people of color are beginning to see clearly how environmental sensitivity, awareness, and action can be linked to their long-standing interest in economic betterment. Environmentalists must rise to the challenge by demonstrating convincingly how environmental and economic progress are linked, and how temporary and artificial is an economic boon that devastates the environment. But more than that, environmentalists must be prepared to advocate sound economics that carry benefits throughout society.

On this point, environmental entrepreneurship offers the hope of a win–win situation, especially to urban dwellers. Well ahead of the entry of major corporate dollars, independent businesspeople are beginning to experiment with and release environmentally sound products into an increasingly receptive marketplace. Urban farms, including aquacultural farms, are beginning to emerge in cities in the Northwest. Environmental entrepreneurs are beginning to illuminate a new path to prosperity; with the right incentives and partnerships, environmentalists and minorities can join together in such efforts, which simultaneously promote environmental awareness, local prosperity, and self-reliance. As environmentalists are becoming increasingly aware, the relationship between prosperity and environmental sensitivity is nearly an iron law: People who are economically deprived and lack a clear sense of security are not apt to embrace much of an environmental agenda, no matter how "appropriately" it is presented. Environmentalists thus must see how vigorously they must work for economic justice and equity before the people they have excluded will begin to listen afresh to the environmental message.

The Special Case of Native Americans

It is crucial to recognize that Indian reservations, unlike other minority communities, possess their own sovereign governments that have long been recognized under laws of the United States. The term *self-determination* thus carries special import for Indian people. With their sovereign status, with powers of taxation, with a series of federal laws and policies encouraging tribal governments to manage the natural resources of their reservations, and with substantial resources to manage, American Indians are uniquely positioned to have significant impacts on environmental issues.

In Indian Country, environmentalists can offer some special assistance. Environmental management is booming on many of the reservations. Tribal programs to regulate water and air quality and enhance wildlife management are rapidly coming to the fore. In the semiarid and arid West, the adjudication of Indian water rights and subsequent tribal use of significant amounts of fresh water are emerging issues with potentially extraordinary consequences. These efforts and programs expand tribal sovereignty into areas formerly controlled by federal and state governments. Since the resources in question are of critical economic importance, sovereignty in these areas has great bearing on the future of the reservations.

Tribal governments need support as they develop various natural resource programs. States that assume management of federally designated environmental programs (such as water-quality management) have traditionally received federal funding in order to proceed; tribal governments also require and deserve such support. Environmentalists can help, first, by coming to understand the magnitude of these issues and programs in Indian Country and, second, by lending a hand (if asked) in seeking congressional and administrative support (or helping to blunt the opposition of offended state agencies who do not want to relinquish regulatory control).

Most environmentalists do not normally list tribal governments when they consider which levels of government they wish to approach with policy alternatives or new environmental programs. They should begin to add tribes to their list, for the reservation lands are significant, and the management of reservation resources offers a new opportunity for creative, pioneering policy in natural resources. Proven tribal interests in preserving biologically critical instream flows in the West are but one example of the ways in which some Indian governments are bringing a new environmental ethic to the management of much-abused resources.

In order to work effectively with tribes, however, environmentalists must realize that the imperatives of Indian self-determination are very strong and that efforts to improve the economies of many Indian reservations will have powerful environmental effects. Native Americans will not naturally choose the path preferred by environmentalists, and they should not be condemned for trying to look after the economic well-being of their people seemingly before environmental quality. This is a case in which understanding, a profound grasp of history, and a breaking of stereotypes on all sides will make for much more effective communication and mutual support among environmental and tribal leaders.

Conclusion

Strategies for forging new links between environmentalists and minorities need to be grounded in the realities of contemporary issues and organizational cultures. Conservationists and environmentalists have made great progress throughout this century precisely because they have remained focused on their own agendas. They cannot be expected to revolutionize their points of view overnight or to jump tracks and land squarely in the center of social justice issues. Nor can environmentalists expect fledgling groups brand new to environmental issues to be instant experts in the technicalities of environmental management. New groups must and will decide for themselves, and in their deciding they will make mistakes, confuse processes with outcomes, and forsake veracity for emotion—in short, they will act just like nearly every venerable conservation group did in its youth. What must be preserved, however, is the people's will to choose. If the electorate cannot be educated, the environmental cause is lost before it begins.

Environmentalists and minority communities beset with environmental problems find themselves in a common struggle. Most environmental problems can be traced to the abuse of power and the concomitant lack of power among large segments of the citizenry. With respect to power, environmentalists must make some hard choices—and they must thus become conscious of their own demands for power and the implications of those demands. Over the long run, they cannot afford the choice of joining in the abuse of power while harboring the illusion that through that means alone they can solve the daunting and egregious problems caused by a deteriorating planetary environment.

If environmental leaders are sincere about diversification, then it is time to reacquaint themselves with the language and mind-set of social justice. Organizations should take great care to evaluate all of their programs, all of their issues both current and in the developmental phase with respect to standards of social justice and equity. Some important questions need to be asked and answered: Who will be served by the organizational goals and objectives? Who might be harmed by them? Are we mindful of the impact of our actions on disenfranchised communities? Are we mindful of the *perceived* as well as the actual impacts? Are there specific ways in which we can involve those communities early on, so that their views and ideas become part of our decision-making process? How can we reflect this increased involvement in social justice so that others will be readily aware of it?

The roots of exclusion in the American conservation-environmental movement reach back to the overt racism prevalent at the turn of the century; they remain watered today through the well-worn habits of largely unconscious organizational behavior. These exclusionary habits will be very hard to change, no matter how much goodwill exists all around. Changes in hiring practices, a necessary first step, will not by themselves eradicate these exclusionary roots (but they will help). The roots of environmental racism run far deeper—well into the institutional soil of the movement. The selection of issues and strategies, the firm reliance on a technical elite to carry most of the load of environmental reform, the avoidance of issues related to social justice and equity, and the emphasis on apparently nonhuman aspects of conservation and environmental issues all mitigate against ready solutions to the dilemma of diversity in the mainstream movement.

The key to diversifying in a manner that is not merely the garnering of token minority representation is for environmental NGOs to become fully conscious of the effects of their patterns of operation. Without meaning to, the great majority of NGOs speak a language that is alien to most minority citizens. The messages they emit are unconsciously tailored to ensure the exclusion of many potential listeners. But the impetus to remain so unconscious will prove to be a very strong one. It has endured, after all, during an entire century of progress among conservation organizations and their issues; it has survived the civil rights movement, the dawning of the "environmental decade" of the seventies, and the enormous growth in international-national environmental organizations. Great risks—or at least the perception of great risks—will accompany genuine strategies to diversify. The will to diversify will be the next great test of the leadership capacities of contemporary conservationists. Will they risk the perception among some of their members that they are gravitating toward issues (or strategies) that "should be" of less concern to them? Will they risk modifying the tried-and-true safety net of their membership demographics?

To zealous environmentalists who are out to save the world from human pillage and greed, these questions may seem incidental, even irrelevant to the progress of their great crusade. But they are not. They are—to paraphrase John Gardner—great opportunities to be greatly met. For conservation leaders today, these questions go to the very heart of principled, progressive leadership.

Notes

1. Peter A. A. Berle, "Saving the World," *Audubon Magazine* (Nov. 1987):6.
2. Stephen Fox, *John Muir and His Legacy: The American Conservation Movement* (Boston: Little, Brown, 1981), 351.
3. Philip Shabecoff, "Environmental Groups Told They Are Racist in Hiring," *New York Times* (February 1, 1990): A16.
4. Samuel P. Hays, *Beauty, Health, and Permanence* (Cambridge: Cambridge University Press, 1987), 14–15.
5. Fox, *John Muir and His Legacy,* 347.
6. Curly Bear Wagner, Blackfeet Tribe Cultural Director, personal communication, July 2, 1990.
7. Fox, *John Muir and His Legacy,* 349.
8. Fox, *John Muir and His Legacy,* 193, 348.
9. Fox, *John Muir and His Legacy,* 195.
10. *Sierra Club Bulletin,* January 1973.
11. Dorceta E. Taylor, "Blacks and the Environment: Toward an Explanation of the Concern and Action Gap Between Blacks and Whites," *Environment and Behavior* 21, no. 2 (March 1989).

12. Taylor, "Blacks and the Environment."
13. Taylor, "Blacks and the Environment."
14. Robert Gottlieb and Helen Ingram, "The New Environmentalists," *The Progressive* (August 1988): 14–15.
15. Gottlieb and Ingram, "The New Environmentalists," 15.
16. Gottlieb and Ingram, "The New Environmentalists."
17. Gottlieb and Ingram, "The New Environmentalists."
18. Lois Marie Gibbs and Karen J. Stults, "On Grassroots Environmentalism," in *Crossroads: Environmental Priorities for the Future,* ed. Peter Borrelli (Washington, D.C.: Island Press, 1988), 241–46. *See also* Gottlieb and Ingram, "The New Environmentalists."
19. Gibbs and Stults, "On Grassroots Environmentalism," 244.
20. Fox, *John Muir and His Legacy,* 349–50.
21. Vawter Parker, "Indians and Environmentalists Drift Apart," *High Country News* (April 1, 1985): 15.

5 Heroines and Hierarchy: Female Leadership in the Conservation Movement

SALLY ANN GUMAER RANNEY
President, American Wildlands

"CALL ME TRIMTAB." These are the words on the gravestone of Buckminster Fuller—three simple words capturing the essence of a life's work and the way Fuller perceived his mission on planet Earth. These words create a metaphor for effective leadership that guided Bucky for over sixty years.

Trim means the readiness of a ship for sailing, or the readiness of a person for action. The *trimtab* is the smallest but perhaps most important steering mechanism on a huge ship. It is a tiny rudder that is part of the main rudder, easily moved in comparison to the main. It will turn the main rudder, which in turn steers the entire ship. Fuller saw himself as a trimtab for "Spaceship Earth," another metaphor he originated that now provides us with a useful, graphic vision of our situation in the universe. His work and concepts push humans *toward* a state of readiness and new ways of thinking, *away* from business as usual in preparation for challenges and events ahead. He was a trimtab and also a captain of concepts.

Effective leadership is essentially about making a difference. It is the ability to see a clear vision of the future and express that vision in a way that others can embrace. The ultimate goal: to shift ideologies and actions and steer history.

Setting aside moral judgments or opinions about their individual visions and actions, one must concede that Attila the Hun and Indira

Gandhi were both effective leaders. In isolated comparison they represent a distinctive balance of fundamental counterpoints of male and female, war and peace, domination and cooperation.

Comprehending the empowerment and sociology of these elemental factors is critical to understanding the evolution of what I call the "genetic psychology" of women in relation to their history in the environmental movement. Only through such a perspective can we chart a future course for dynamic female leadership in conservation.

Female Socialization

In a keynote speech addressing the assembly of the 4th World Wilderness Congress in September of 1987, Oren R. Lyons, Chief of the Onondaga Nation, stated that the earth is in peril because women, until very recent history, have been devalued, diminished, or altogether eliminated during important decision-making processes. The effect is a planet out of balance and in peril. Chief Lyons' provocative remarks prompt a series of questions.

Was the exclusion of women an accident of history, a social miscarriage that repeated itself time and time again, or an evolutionary process that could not be accelerated or bypassed? Is there a contemporary trend toward more female leadership in social and political movements—and, for the purposes of this discussion particularly, the conservation movement—or are women who surface in keystone positions just temporary blips on the screen of events?

Why are there not more female "trimtabs" and captains steering the conservation movement at the national level? What works for and against women striving to be conservation leaders? What kinds of leadership roles will be needed in the future in conservation, and what are the readiness requirements? How can women position themselves in order to make a significant difference in the environmental movement?

What are the costs and rewards of leadership service? Are managerial and inspirational leadership one and the same? Do contemporary hierarchies perpetuate or submerge heroine potential?

To address these questions, we must first explore the socialization of women over the course of history and their role in our society. Sandra Lin Marburg's "Women and the Environment: Subsistence Paradigms 1850–1950" submits two gender-related paradigms that she uses as structural frameworks. These paradigms, relevant to both Western and non-Western societies, associate men with culture and women with nature. The "ethnographic paradigm emphasizes the interdependencies between the sexes while the economic paradigm emphasizes male dominance."

The ethnographic paradigm is useful in defining the functioning roles of men and women, particularly in prehistory. Women as nature were primarily maternal. Men as culture were hunters and providers. Marburg argues that early researchers significantly underestimated the value of the substantial role of females as providers of vegetable foods in gatherer-hunter cultures, as well as collectors of fuel and water, gatherers and preparers of clothing materials, and manufacturers of tools, carrying and cooking vessels. Yet the division of labor between the sexes was perceived as productive. Woman and man needed each other as partners for survival.

The economic paradigm explains industrialized societies of "male centrism, productive domains and the inclusion of women only as they fit into those frameworks."

It was not until the nineteenth century that an "exaggerated duality of innate sex differences" appeared and a predominantly economic paradigm emerged. "Women were portrayed as material and conservative, men as intellectual and progressive," Marburg explains. The domestic economy became separate from the political economy. Women's work was perceived as nonproductive because it was unpaid. With the systematic exclusion of women, industrialized society became increasingly male-centered. Male centrism meant male domination over nature, and women represented nature. Woman's relationship to man became based on economic dependency. Her relationships with other women were competitive in order to capture the best provider in marriage. Literal interpretations of Christian doctrine also assisted in perpetuating the perception of man's dominion over the earth, over all other creatures and that which was natural.

Over time this created what Marburg describes as a "universal imagery" of women and new paradigms of livelihood. Women were maternal, yes, but also passive, unproductive, and dependent. They were the "interior sex." Men were active, aggressive, functioning, and productive—the "exterior sex."

Women have been laboring under this imagery and socialization process for centuries. Even though great strides have been made recently to dissolve some of women's societal stigmas, subtle rumblings continue to work deep in women's behavior. Consequently, women are unconscious victims of socialization flashbacks.

The research of Carol Gilligan (1982) on the moral development of women supports Marburg's paradigms. Gilligan consistently found that men describe themselves in terms of great ideas, distinctive activity, and individual achievement. Their moral development is predicated on a hierarchy of rules and rights. They perceive their relationships through positioning and distribution of power and authority. Women define themselves more in terms of relationships and responsibilities, caring and compassion, support and nonaggression.

Outspoken, cause-motivated, and economically productive women were the exception, not the rule. They participated as "allowed" by men on the periphery of the economic and political system and under great cultural restraints, male biases, and frustration. The suffrage movement brought women collectively into direct conflict with political economies for the first time. The conservation movement was progressing during the same period. The exposure to the political climate of the day in both movements clearly expanded the effectiveness of women for the cause of natural resource protection in America. In spite of male centrism, women were pivotal forces behind many victories even though historians and researchers (the majority of whom were male until a surge of feminist scholarship in the 1970s) washed lightly over their accomplishments and contributions.

The 1960s and 1970s saw a dramatic escalation in the race toward female empowerment. Mobilization for passage of the Equal Rights Amendment was key. As Joyce Kelly (1986) says in an article about women as change agents, the battle for equal opportunity has been fought and mostly won. Sex discrimination is now more subtle and in some ways more difficult to ascertain and overcome even though the changes women have made in the work force are a power with which to be reckoned.

Jennifer James of the Department of Behavioral Science at the University of Washington takes the investigation of male and female differences further. She maintains that people do not make the majority of their decisions about sex roles in a logical way. Decisions are based on personal experience, emotion, history, and culture—"anything that maximizes the defense mechanisms" (James 1983).

Finding balance between male and female is now the dilemma for women, particularly in the professional world. They are consistently caught between the new approach of confidence, efficiency, determination, commitment, and independence and the old style of being needed, sexually seductive, and dependent. It is a seemingly eternal paradox.

James also indicates that men are better risk takers, depersonalize conflict, and are more independent. Women personalize conflict because so much of their discord throughout history was deeply emotional, rooted as it was in family and intimate relationships. Consequently, women prefer to avoid conflict.

Men are better team players because of sports training and participation. Women are not generally team-oriented and are less able to collaborate with other women. James suggests this is a modern social phenomenon brought on in the aftermath of World War II. A woman's whole life, socially and economically, depended on one decision: whom she married. Women had to compete with other women for the few "elite men" who could take care of them and "make their life beautiful," secure, and comfortable. In the female psyche, this situation truly became a matter akin to life and death.

To carry Kelly's thesis further, James suggests that women in the professional world are consistently being asked to neutralize femininity. Women are taught not only to wear their mothers' clothes but their fathers' as well. She points out the example of a female banker "dressed for success." In order to achieve position in the ranks, she should wear a navy blue, black, or brown double-breasted suit. Cut off at the knees, it is clearly not male, but it isn't female either. It is, however, nonthreatening. It makes a female banker look like a "little male banker," someone whom the male hierarchy perceives as competent, credible, and businesslike.

With so many mixed signals, women have difficulty asserting themselves without personal penalty. Reviewing feminine history, one can easily see why women first surfaced in the world outside the domestic economy in cause-related activities, volunteer work, and charities. Here, they were free to express other dimensions of female identity and, although cautiously, design their own playing field. Yet even in the retreat of female volunteerism, women still dangled from hierarchical strings held exclusively by men.

Understanding female socialization provides insight into the contemporary challenges facing women both in their personal and professional lives. As related to conservation, both a cause-related and professional platform, this insight opens the window far enough that we can begin to recognize the reasons for the scarcity of female leadership and what is needed to foster more of it. Ironically, the conservation movement in this country truly began as a women's movement.

Women and the History of American Conservation

There is a long tradition of women's natural history literature as well as female conservation activism in America. Through some of the early writings of women, we can see the first glimmer of conservation and preservation concern.

Two women in particular are noteworthy because they were widely read. Born in England in 1831, Isabella Bird traveled to the United States to explore the Rocky Mountains in 1873. By no means the first female tourist, she was at the time perhaps the most articulate. This resulted in the publication of *A Lady's Life in the Rocky Mountains* in 1878, a collection of letters to her sister. Her goal was "simply to experience the place the same as any male nature lover." She relished the adventure and its challenges, loving the alpine country and its seasons. She recognized that her civilized ways, the motivation causing her to seek the wild, were also the very thing that threatened it. Bird saw the wilderness as "a place of freedom from civilization, never doubting that civilization would overtake the wilds. She did not see the possibility of a relationship, other than that based on challenge, between man and nature" (Norwood 1984).

Mary Hunter Austin, on the other hand, cherished the desert. She wrote not so much of its magnitude, but of how each detail of life in the desert contributes to the whole. *Land of Little Rain,* Austin's most famous work, has become a classic in American nature writing. Unlike Bird, Austin believed it possible for civilized persons to accept the wilderness without trampling it, but a change of attitude was required. There must be a "certain defeat of pride . . . a humility . . . in her culture before it can accept the requirements of life in the wilderness" (Norwood 1984).

According to Peter Wild (1979), Austin set the stage for Aldo Leopold, Joseph Wood Krutch, Edward Abbey, and others who wrote with sensitivity about human-nature relationships—and most particularly about the Southwest. A conservation activist as well as author, individualist, and mystic, Austin wrote that "not the law but the land sets limits." The governor of New Mexico appointed her to a board that was considering construction of the Hoover Dam. She served until she discovered that the board had been stacked with dam supporters, then quit in disgust. Assertive and well-positioned in society, she had liberal access to the celebrities of her day. She used her flair and determination cunningly for the benefit of conservation and feminist causes.

During the progressive movement of conservation at the turn of the century, the role of women as environmental protectors blossomed. The first conservation priority for women became the preservation of forests in the face of "hell-bent-for-leather" logging. Perhaps the most recognized, but not the most influential, of these early female conservationists was Gifford Pinchot's mother, Mrs. James Pinchot, who chaired the Conservation Committee of the 77,000-member Daughters of the American Revolution.

The Conservation Committee was actively involved in protection efforts for Niagara Falls, the Palisades of the Hudson, and watersheds

of the Appalachian Mountains. When the committee wrote to governors asking how they could best serve the cause of conservation,
they were told, as reported by Mrs. Jay Cooke Howard, that "most
of the governors preferred to have us turn our attention to children
rather than to the men." The virtues of teaching children conservation, along with obedience, patriotism, cleanliness, and truth, were
then recounted in the DAR newsletter.

The insatiable fashion demand for feathers in the late 1800s pushed
egrets, swallows, terns, and orioles toward extinction. Editorials in
Field and Stream called for legislation to protect plumed birds. It was
the urgency of this issue that prompted the organizing of the first
Audubon societies, which grew to 30,000 members almost overnight. The growth declined as quickly as it mushroomed, but three
years later under the leadership of Mabel Wright, the various societies
banded together under the auspices of the publication *Bird Lore.*

By 1913 the practice of putting feathers on hats was all but
stopped. A tariff act prohibiting imports of wild bird feathers passed
because of the unceasing efforts of the Audubon societies and the
General Federation of Women's Clubs. A monumental victory for
Audubon, it established the organization as a major conservation
force.

Even as Audubon gained strength with over half of its membership
comprised of women, men held nearly all of the official positions.
Because of its alliances with sportsmen, however, the society often
hesitated to take action on issues critical to comestible wildlife. This
fact came to the attention of one of Audubon's life members, a zealous conservation amateur named Rosalie Edge. As she investigated
Audubon's ties to sportsmen's groups, she became enraged at what
she called a morally corrupt organization of dishonest action. She
founded the Emergency Conservation Council for the sole purpose
of attacking her beloved Audubon Society.

Having cut her activist teeth in the suffrage movement, Edge was
an astute observer of male character. She quickly learned to match
wits with men and use her femininity to extract important information or make a point. From her days in the suffrage movement she
had learned how to create visibility on the outside to force reform

internally. Her disclosures to the membership of the society's inner workings and finances revealed deception and mismanagement on the part of its officials and President Gilbert Pearson. Her target was as much Pearson the president as it was Pearson the good-old-boy hunter and chameleon conservationist. His chauvinism did not daunt Edge, but his position favoring predator extinction and his misuse of funds infuriated her. A passionate and articulate champion of these issues, she magnetized a good portion of Audubon's membership to her side. With pit-bull persistence, she eventually succeeded. Pearson was dislodged. The battle cost Audubon membership, which rebounded in time, and launched Edge into a position of great influence as a New Deal conservationist. She is perhaps without peer for her fire and honesty as keeper of Audubon's conscience during her long tenure. Historian Stephen Fox (1981) uses Edge as his leading example of the "enlightened amateur" who has always been a vital force in American conservation.

Another outstanding amateur conservationist was Mrs. Lovell White, who founded the California Woman's Club in 1897 in response to the aborted California suffrage campaign. Combining membership with other women's clubs in 1900, it became the California Federation of Women's Clubs.

In the same year, the federation president, Mrs. Robert Burdett, announced:

> While the women of New Jersey are saving the Palisades of the Hudson from utter destruction by men to whose greedy souls Mount Sinai is only a stone quarry, and the women of Colorado are saving the cliff dwellings and pueblo ruins of their state from vandal destruction, the word comes to the women of California that men whose souls are gang-saws are meditating the turning of our world-famous Sequoias into planks and fencing worth so many dollars. . . . Better one living tree in California, than fifty acres of lumberyard. Preserve and replant them and the State will be blessed a thousand fold in the development of its natural resources. . . . (Merchant 1984)

She went on to say that forests were the source of the state's waters and that the health of the state's people and the comfort of their homes were made possible by these resources. Thus began one of the most colorful, hard-fought conservation battles in the West. It was not until 1954 and three federation presidents later that those groves identified for preservation in the early 1900s were fully protected.

The establishment of Big Basin State Park to protect another species of redwood is also credited to the forceful Mrs. Lovell White. Under her guidance, the Save the Redwoods League was founded on a membership of both men and women. The organization is still active today and is credited with many later additions to Redwood National Park.

The California Federation of Women's Clubs was also responsible for legislation that established a school of forestry at the University of California in Berkeley, a precedent carried forward by women's clubs in several other states including Pennsylvania.

Forestry battles continued to rage across the country. In Minnesota, Lydia Phillips Williams mobilized a movement to save the Chippewa Forest Reserve from what she called the "Board Feet" mentality. This involved an appeal of the "Dead and Down Timber Act" and required sending women to Washington to meet with congressmen.

Harriet West Jackson led the successful fight to save the famous Calaveras Groves. Women's clubs in Florida were creating forest preserves, while Maine's clubs established Katahdin State Forest. *The Directory of Historical Trees* came out of the Massachusetts club. The General Federation of Women's Clubs' Forestry Committee skillfully guided passage of the Weeks Bill, which protected watersheds of navigable streams.

In 1909 Mrs. John Wilkinson of Louisiana formed the Waterways Committee to promote cleaner, cheaper water and water development. The rationale for protecting both forests and waterways was to conserve the health of the American home.

The General Federation of Women's Clubs developed into an 800,000-member organization, with *Century* magazine as its organ. The influence and clout of its Forestry Committee played a vital role in the conservation of forests, bird life, and waterways.

The only woman invited to the White House for the Governors' Conference on Conservation in 1908 was federation president Sarah

Platt Decker of Denver. In the same year, Lydia Williams wrote an article called "Conservation—Women's Work." The article lamented the fact that men do not consider future generations; they are "too busy building railroads, constructing ships, engineering great projects and exploiting vast commercial enterprises." Williams' theme was that "man the moneymaker had left it to the woman the money saver to preserve resources" (Merchant 1984).

A benchmark year, 1908 also witnessed the founding of the Women's National Rivers and Harbors Congress, the female counterpart of Josephe E. Ransdell's National Rivers and Harbors Congress. It gained 20,000 members in fourteen months. One of its most renowned achievements was a bill to protect Niagara Falls from water developers. The Rivers and Harbors Congress also pushed for the cleanup of streams and shorelines and assigned women to churches in various communities to lecture on conservation's "moral standpoints."

Carolyn Merchant writes: "[Women] repeatedly called on the traditions assigned them by society in justifying the public demands they were making. Unwilling and unable to break out of these social roles, and supported by the men of the National Conservation Congresses, they drew on a trilogy of slogans—conservation of womanhood, the home and the child" (Merchant 1984).

Women were speaking out for conservation, but the lack of access to the polls limited their influence and frustrated them greatly. Pushed by its members and primarily its Forestry Committee, the General Federation of Women's Clubs took a position on suffrage late in the movement.

Kate Gordon, vice president of the National American Women's Suffrage Association, addressed the federation in 1910: "We have never had a democracy, we have only had a sex oligarchy and . . . there are some men and some women who are not satisfied with existing conditions. . . . We don't want a man-made world; we don't want a woman-made world, but we want a world where the opinions of men and women rate equally and then, and not till then, will we have a true democracy!" (Merchant 1984).

The suffrage movement finally succeeded in its goal. But in 1913 the conservation activism of women received a deadly blow. *American Forestry,* the magazine of the American Forestry Association, covered the Fifth National Conservation Congress in Washington, D.C. In the photographs of some fifty committees and 160 men seated at speakers' tables, not one woman appeared although many attended. The absence of women was explained away with a statement that the congress was attended by men who were "no longer in need of general educational propaganda relative to conservation of natural resources, but attended the Congress for the purpose of meeting progressive men in their own and related lines to secure specific information helpful in the solution of their own problems . . . where active workers desire an opportunity to exchange views on technical problems . . ." (Merchant 1984).

This event signaled the arrival of conservation and forestry as technical professions. Women were excluded. Articles about women in forestry disappeared, along with Lydia Williams.

The event that probably precipitated this exclusion was the parting of ways between the General Federation of Women's Clubs and Gifford Pinchot over Hetch Hetchy Dam. Always a supporter of the federation's Conservation Committee, Pinchot sided with San Francisco when it proposed a referendum in 1908 to build the dam. John Muir took the issue to the nation; women took it to the steps of the Capitol. The San Francisco city engineer called the dam's opponents "short-haired women and long-haired men," an image that stuck with environmentalists right through what I call the "braided armpit" syndrome of the 1960s and 1970s. A congressional representative from the San Francisco area wrote to Pinchot saying that the campaign against the dam was mobilized by "misinformed nature lovers."

Hetch Hetchy was lost, but the nation awakened. Women were still active in conservation, but the country didn't know it. The Sierra Club's outings program offered women the opportunity to experience the wilderness. By 1915, over half of Audubon's members were women. The National Parks Association had more female members than male in 1929.

This early history of women's activism set a subtle tone to which female leadership in conservation has resonated over the past six decades. There were a few campaigns during the 1930s and 1940s, although activities dropped off dramatically because of preoccupation with the depression, the Dust Bowl, and World War II. Conservation concerns were more in the context of conserving fuel and other resources for the war effort than in preserving landscapes.

It was not until the early 1960s, when Rachel Carson published *Silent Spring,* that America was catapulted into an environmental alert. Carson's unidealized descriptions of the insidious and obvious dangers of pesticides reignited recognition of women as conservation leaders and the importance of environmental protection and management. She alerted both men and women to the urgent biological imperatives resulting from pollution. Reviewers and readers alike found it incredible that a woman could produce a "scientific" book, not realizing that ten years earlier she had written *The Sea Around Us.*

Carson was the first to articulate what subsequently became one of Garrett Hardin's ecological principles: "The more we know, the less sure we are of our knowledge . . . and the more we need to know." Although expressed later by others, she introduced the concept that if we are to err, we had best err on the side of conservation.

With Rachel Carson came a new wave of remarkable and dedicated women in conservation. A few attained national stature. Margaret Owings of California was instrumental in getting watersheds critical to Redwood National Park (as well as the sea otter and the mountain lion) protected. Mardy Murie, one of the first white women to visit Alaska and the wife of wildlife biologist Olaus Murie, worked unceasingly for passage of the Wilderness Act and the Alaska Lands Conservation Act. Celia Hunter, pilot and pioneer, helped form the first citizen conservation organization in Alaska and took the state's issues to Washington. Katie Lee—author, singer, river runner and activist—was deeply involved in the battle to save the Glen Canyon from construction of Glen Canyon Dam. Lady Bird Johnson, perhaps the only first lady to make conservation one of her personal priorities, worked to protect the wilderness and biological diversity. Peggy Wayburn, a longtime presence in the Sierra Club and the wife of one of its foremost leaders, Dr. Edgar Wayburn, has been active in issues ranging from wilderness to energy policy.

All are now in their sixties, seventies, or eighties and are truly conservation heroines of the first order. They represent a resilient, vanishing breed of women of the last generation. Their personal stories are riveted with hardship and humor, inspiration and an unflinching dedication to nature. In reviewing their lives, one can detect many common denominators. Each is well grounded in her relationship with nature through repeated personal experience in the wild outdoors. Each is an inspirational national leader working outside the system (except for Lady Bird Johnson) in order to achieve her goals. None was a trained professional in the usual sense. All have been involved in some other form of public service beyond the cause of conservation, and for each it has been a lifelong commitment and labor of love. All are eternal optimists.

To whom does the baton pass and what must the next generation of women do to prepare themselves to be the trimtabs and captains of "Spaceship Earth"?

Change and Challenge

There is a disconcerting timelessness about conservation. The issues never seem to die. Objectives and concerns overall are the same whether the cause is saving a species or fighting pollution, yet each issue has a different face masked with various political, economic, and social considerations. In many cases, the losses are forever. The art of delay can mean victory, and victories must be won over and over before they are secure.

In the last thirty years we have evolved, as David Brower says, into a society that is subservient to technology. In the process, conservation (the preservation, protection, and responsible use of resources) has been magnified dramatically to include environmentalism (the protection of environmental quality, functioning ecosystems, air, and water from toxic pollution and mismanagement).

One of the first contemporary environmental issues to experience the energy and enthusiasm of female leadership is the issue of toxics and hazardous wastes. Just as women of the progressive conservation movement of the early 1900s were sensitive to the protection of forests and waters in order to preserve the quality of their homes, so are contemporary women attuned to the threats that pollution and hazardous wastes hold for family and personal health.

Lois Gibbs of the Citizens' Clearinghouse for Hazardous Wastes (CCHW) testifies to the compelling grass-roots leadership of women in these issues. Helping to coordinate efforts in over 4,000 communities, she asserts that the reason there have been no sitings of new hazardous waste facilities in this country in the past ten years is not because of Congress or professional lobbyists haunting the halls of Congress, but because of the power of spontaneous, "unprofessional" leadership in communities, the majority of which is female. Some of these women are surfacing as leaders at the state level with coaching and leadership training from Gibbs's organization. Yet on the national horizon, Gibbs and only a small handful of others are visible.

In land use, forestry, and wildlife resources, women also constitute a significant minority. In 1987 Stephen Kellert and Joyce Berry published the results of their in-depth study "Attitudes, Knowledge and Behaviors Toward Wildlife as Affected by Gender," which provides meaningful insights into this dilemma. Their findings are consistent with the research of Carol Gilligan regarding male and female socialization.

Kellert and Berry found that men endorsed exploitation of wildlife or the usurpation of wildlife habitat to yield increased material gains to human society. Males viewed wildlife more in terms of whether populations can sustain particular levels of harvest. In general they had more knowledge of wildlife anatomy because they also had more direct contact with wild animals through hunting, trapping, and fishing.

Women value animals differently. They have a great affinity toward pets, but relate to remote, unfamiliar wild animals in a more detached manner. They are more concerned about animal welfare. Women are generally less knowledgeable on wildlife issues, such as the coyote-sheep or steel-versus-lead-shot controversies. Men predominantly belong to sportmen's organizations, while 62 percent of the women in the study belong to environmental protection organizations and 80 percent belong to animal protection groups.

These are clearly colliding gender variations that permeate resource management approaches as well as professional hierarchies. The predominant view of how the world works is based on male imagery.

One conclusion Kellert and Berry drew from their study is that dominance and control (male) versus mutuality, support, and relationship (female) influence traditionally held styles of thought and management within natural resource and wildlife bureaucracies. The predominant male approach is alien to many aspiring female professionals, constituting a subtle bias against those entering the field. In 1985 four and a half percent of all those in the forestry profession were women. Thirty-eight percent of the work force in wildlife agencies is women. However, only 8 percent are in higher-level positions, while over 80 percent of the lower-level positions are held by women. In 1986 25 percent of all students enrolled in wildlife and forestry were women, but if recent history is a reliable guide, the increasing numbers of women in training as resource professionals will not translate into significantly greater numbers of women managing natural resource agencies.

Female Leadership: Personal Reflections

What do leaders do that makes them successful?

That question has far-reaching implications for women in conservation, given the female socialization processes and the nature of natural resource issues, bureaucracies, and organizational structures. A great deal depends on individual experiences and how one views the world and one's own circumstances.

Senator Everett Dirksen said he was a "man of principles whose first principle is flexibility." In my experience, flexibility is fundamental to the effective and successful leadership of women in conservation. Flexibility is an attitude, not a condition. It is learned over time through practice. Conservation was not a premeditated educational career move for me. I stumbled into it through the back door, and a swinging back door at that, which eventually led to a presidential appointment. I chose a small liberal arts college in the Colorado mountains over Stanford for its proximity to skiing and cowboys. At the age of nineteen, I determined that my destiny was to paint western landscapes, teach secondary school, dabble in geology and music, rodeo a little and ski a lot, marry a cowboy and live happily ever after on a ranch in the Rockies—all of which I did manage to fit into a sliver of seven years.

A career in conservation and environmentalism was not even remotely in my life's plan. In the beginning, conservation registered emotionally through how I *felt* about indiscriminate clear-cutting in my backyard, wild creatures losing their wilderness, and the wilderness losing its wildness. I felt angry when pelicans strangled in six-pack plastic and poisoned eagles were stacked five high in frozen piles for counting. I was utterly mystified when magical desert canyons, millions of years in the making, were disemboweled on a prayer for the glimmer of gold or uranium. I was deeply hurt when a very special, personal place I adopted as my own in the forest was to be logged.

When the great blue herons migrated through the family ranch in spring, we felt privileged to witness, if only for a day or two, their path of eternal homecoming. At the river's edge I found the rhythm of nature's resolve. In the wilderness I was inspired by the miracle of simply being and the solitude that allowed the inspiration to spring forth.

One winter a female bobcat kept her cubs under our ranch house bathroom floor. My first house was a four-room cabin shared with six Siberian husky sled dogs. Many full-mooned winter nights, the air so cold and clear it hung like a frozen curtain of glass splinters, we'd turn out the lights, throw back our heads, and howl. Within minutes coyotes would answer, and one of the most primeval of all nature's duets was in full chorus.

Living on a ranch calmed and grounded me. I became heart-connected to nature and value-connected to conservation although I did not recognize that until many years later. When I did, the realization allowed me to take risks in my personal and professional life and perceive adversity and conflict as stepping-stones instead of stumbling blocks. Living in a small-town, rural setting yet not being bound by the inbred tradition of lifelong residents also provided a perfect opportunity to experiment with male hierarchies without jeopardizing my interests or career.

The Roadless Area Review and Evaluation in the early 1970s, along with the dismantling of the National Timber Supply Act, exposed me to the technical, political, and policy sides of conservation. A greenhorn at grass-roots organizing, I suddenly found myself in Forest Service files, on the front porches of my neighbors, and in the halls of Congress, learning bottom-up and top-down approaches to influencing public land and environmental policy. Living in a pluralistic society provides tremendous opportunity for citizens to influence what happens. When not involved, we accept by default whatever transpires.

The Wilderness Society offered me an employment contract that I accepted after much anguish over leaving my life-style in the mountains. I determined there was more opportunity to influence policy through an organization than as an independent agent. I went to work in the society's regional office in Denver. There I found two mentors of extraordinary vision, knowledge, and dedication to conservation who taught me politics and professionalism.

But my tenure there was shortened to only a few years. An organizational crisis led to the closing of the western regional office. I turned down the position of director of the society's lobbying staff in Washington, D.C., preferring life for myself and my small son in proximity to the West's rivers and mountains. I also believed firmly in the power of the grass roots and feared the myopia that can result from life on the Potomac. My decision to bypass the new job required a reassessment of my commitment to conservation and my own goals within the movement.

Because of my past experiences and socialization, I believe that accomplishment is born of risk, of the courage to step beyond what's comfortable, predictable, or known. I also believe that one must take charge of one's own destiny. Thus I joined some comrades and with $100 of what I called "ad-venture capital" we founded the American Wilderness Alliance, now called American Wildlands. It has been a launching pad for my conservation work ever since.

The AWA immediately propelled me into another dimension of conservation. It demanded leadership abilities and managerial skills simply in order to survive. Being lean meant being resourceful and finding inner strengths that otherwise might never have been tapped. It offered the chance to design a hierarchy instead of being assigned to someone else's, to play the game on my own terms without being submerged in a bureaucracy.

It is extremely important for women to look much more closely than men at their own personal socialization process in relation to leadership positions in conservation. A cause-related profession, conservation demands a steady, deep resolve and inner grounding in order to survive the hurdles and make it *through* and *around* the male hierarchy. Self-examination can make the difference between being a "sustainer" or becoming an "achiever," between taking the well-beaten path or choosing "the road less travelled."

Mine was only one path. There are several outstanding women in the leadership ranks of conservation, but on the national scene only a small fraction in comparison to men. A few of these contemporaries include Joan Martin-Brown of the United Nation Environmental Programme; Joyce Kelly, executive director of the Wildlife Habitat Enhancement Council; Anne LaBastille, ecologist, author, and woodswoman; Dr. Cheryl Charles, director of Project Wild; Frances Beinecke, former president of The Wilderness Society; Maggi Fox, southwestern regional director of the Sierra Club; Sherri Griffith, river outfitter and former president of Western River Guides Association; Scootch Pankonin, secretary of American Rivers; Jean Hocker, president of the Land Trust Alliance; Kathryn Fuller, president of the World Wildlife Fund and The Conservation Foundation; and Joanna Underwood, president of INFORM, Inc.

Female CEOs are almost nonexistent among the major national

conservation groups. This reveals not only something about the direction in which the conservation movement is headed, but also about organizational structure.

The stunning complexity of contemporary conservation issues is partly responsible for pushing the national movement away from the grass-roots and toward greater technical specialization. Managerial leadership is in greater demand than inspirational leadership, a phenomenon not unique to conservation, but apparent in the evolution of many social movements including civil rights and women's rights.

One of the reasons for the scarcity of female leadership in national conservation is not only the subtle barriers inherent in male-dominated hierarchies, but the difficulty women have in ascertaining early on how the hierarchy functions, particularly beneath the surface. Male *perceptions* dominate regardless of what seems to be intended or verbalized. Women must be aware of what bearing this has on their own grounding, socialization, and leadership goals. A thoughtful assessment of these factors will help eliminate dead ends, unwelcome surprises, and frustration.

Another reason for the scarcity of national female leadership is that the career costs to women in leadership roles are greater than those for men. Because cause-related work is not a nine-to-five job, women are in a position of constantly having to choose between jobs and home, dancing between male and female roles and courting chronic fatigue. As a consequence, many women eventually surrender themselves to sustainer roles. Because it takes time to filter upward in a hierarchy, older, experienced women may be more reluctant to take on leadership roles: They are often wiser about the price of sacrificing families, personal relationships, and free time.

Elements of Successful Conservation Leadership for Women

The imperatives for future leadership by women, particularly of the next generation, have more dimensions than they did in the past.

Writing in *Windstar Journal* (1987), Marshall Thurber and Ron Kaufman identify three elements that are critical to successful leadership in the future: vision, frequency of interaction, and metaphors.

VISION

Successful leaders have a clear vision of the way things should be. They communicate that vision simply so that others can see it and participate. They have optimism and carry "a brightness of the future."

This approach includes a personal vision (creative visualization). A woman must visualize who she wants to be and what she wants to accomplish.

Because women suffer from unconscious socialization flashbacks, their general tendency is to undervalue themselves. It then becomes difficult to visualize themselves as trimtabs or captains, regardless of merit or credentials. This in itself, particularly in highly competitive organizational structures, automatically spells "stalled."

FREQUENCY OF INTERACTION

Leaders are not afraid to have consistent and positive interaction with constituents, coworkers, employees, the press, or anyone else with whom the vision needs to be shared. This dictates a conscious effort at visibility. Visibility within the conservation movement often means more responsibility and accountability, honed public relations skills, and more travel. As all the research shows, with more nonaggressive socialization than males, women are generally more hesitant about creating visibility for themselves.

METAPHORS

Effective metaphors shift perceptions. Fuller's metaphor "Spaceship Earth" transformed our perception of human relationships to one another and the planet. Metaphors are simple and use clear imagery. Women tend to use natural metaphors, while men's are often mechanical. Metaphors will be extremely important in galvanizing support for future environmental issues because they can move political leaders and millions of followers to act quickly.

I see additional skills and characteristics that will affect the leadership imperatives for women in the future of conservation. These go beyond understanding female and personal socialization processes and how they influence leadership abilities and goals. My observations, experiences, and mistakes precipitated the following twenty Guideposts to the Leadership Labyrinth. I hope these loose-leaf rules will help women chart a character and disciplinary course that will increase the odds of achieving leadership in what will be a vastly expanded and more complex conservation movement of the future.

Guideposts to the Leadership Labyrinth

1. Be passionate about personal commitment to conservation. Have a strong relationship with the natural world through direct and repeated experiences that renew energy and dedication.
2. Develop an attitude of adventure and a willingness to take risks; be prepared to opt out of security and into uncertainty in order to accelerate growth, accomplishment, and learning. Be flexible.
3. Develop a world view. Live the metaphor of acting locally but thinking globally. Be involved in the world peace movement. Environmental quality and distribution of natural resources will ultimately create further peril or bring security to the planet. It will be important to know the key players and issues.
4. Develop team skills. Be willing to climb into the male psyche in order to learn its strengths and weaknesses and understand locker-room mentality and lunch-box etiquette. The success of cause-related movements depends on effective organizing and politicking. Training in team sports is one of the single most important skills a woman can have to be a successful leader.
5. Make a conscious effort to educate the left and right side of the brain by including both scientific and aesthetic components in training and formal education. Maintain a fine-tuned balance between intuitive knowledge and intellectual knowledge.
6. Avoid advanced technical specialization. Integrators and gen-

eralists who are also inspirational leaders will be the trimtabs and captains. Experts can always be found to fill in the gaps.

7. Create an individual identity and style of leadership and management that optimizes strengths and minimizes weaknesses.

8. Understand and be skilled in using computer technology and advanced information systems. The currency of conservation is information. John Naisbitt's *Megatrends* outlines changes in power structures that will occur with increased computer technology and communications systems. These can be powerful assets for the conservation movement.

9. Train in negotiations. The environmental movement has gradually changed its approach from head-on collision to cooperative convergence. I wish all women leaders could take a course in negotiations from Henry Kissinger.

10. Find a mentor and be willing to mentor in return in later years. Studies show that most leaders have mentors along their career paths. They also reveal that women are less receptive to mentors than men. Mentoring provides continuity and cohesiveness, insights and guidance that are hard to come by in any other way. The corporate world has used this principle for decades.

11. Learn to win and play to win, using systems and common denominators instead of personal justifications, prejudices, or biases. This applies to all kinds of systems, including organizational, hierarchical, political, social, and economic systems.

12. Identify role models. The most useful approach is to choose several role models, each of whom embodies a characteristic or achievement that relates to personal goals and ideals. I have thirteen role models, each with a distinctive quality to which I can aspire. They include Georgia O'Keeffe, because of her genius of simplicity, independence, and artistry; Gro Harlem Brundtland, former prime minister of Norway, because of her negotiation skills in chairing the Global Commission on the Environment; Mardy Murie, for her quiet power and deep commitment to wilderness; Beryl Markham, pilot and author of *West with the Night,* because of her spirit of adventure; wild-

life biologist Dian Fossey, for her resolve over all odds; political activist Barbara Marx Hubbard, because of her vision of the future; Eleanor Roosevelt, for her political skills and ability to "lead from behind"; and Stephen Hawking, the finest mental athlete of our time.

13. Learn the basics of Spanish, Russian, and economics. Predictions indicate a good third of the United States will be speaking Spanish by the year 2005; citizen diplomacy exchanges will explode between the USSR and the U.S.A. The global environment will become a priority. With the coming convergence of economics and conservation, those knowledgeable in both will have vast opportunities to participate and lead.

14. Fine-tune communication skills; learn to write and speak well.

15. Strive to be a "longhouse thinker." The longhouse was the structure built by many Native American and aboriginal peoples where the long-term plans, universal contemplations, and major decisions of the tribe took place. Becoming a longhouse thinker means stretching one's vision to the farthest reaches of great achievement. Conceiving of and implementing the space program made John F. Kennedy a longhouse thinker.

16. Learn about metaphysics. The world is rapidly approaching a renaissance that will meld science and spirit. Whether one subscribes to it is not the question, but knowing the essence of this new wave of thinking will be important because it will affect power structures, politics, and human relations in the future.

17. Study the ancient martial art of aikido. It is a training in positional thinking and how to use one's own energy as effortlessly as possible in relation to opposing energy. Its concepts of strength are effective and very different from traditional Western paradigms because it minimizes polarization. There is "magic in conflict" if the principles of conflict are understood. Conservation issues are by nature full of conflict. For women leading the field, understanding their socialization with respect to conflict can make them more powerful and effective.

18. Understand crisis management in order to avoid it, but recognize the opportunity in chaos.
19. Understand that great changes in human thinking must occur in this and the next generation if humans are to find solutions to environmental problems of unimaginable difficulty, consequence, and magnitude that have no historical precedent.
20. Develop a sense of humor and keep a close rein on ego. Remember, you're not here for a long time, you're here for a good time.

Telescope into the Future

The challenges ahead lie not so much in identifying the agenda, which will be dictated by events such as global warming and threats to biodiversity, but in shifting the world political system into equilibrium, as Dr. Paul Ehrlich and Senator Albert Gore affirm. This requires more female leadership throughout the system in order to balance male dominance. The opportunities are extraordinary. Environment and natural resources are rapidly coming to match national security and world economics in importance. Women must be willing and prepared to serve.

From what quarters will the next generation of conservation heroines come?

Some will arrive from other social movements, including world peace and hunger, migrating into conservation as the planet deteriorates. At the community level, women will continue to rise to the occasion—ordinary people doing extraordinary things. Some will leap from the legal to the environmental field. Others will rebound from recreation and tourism into conservation. An unseeming alliance only ten years ago, recreation and conservation are beginning to grow together partly through a convergence with increased travel and telecommunications. All four of these fields are reducing the size of the globe and expanding our world view. Tourist economies are quickly becoming a viable economic opportunity for protecting natural systems (eco-tourism) and bringing all peoples closer to world peace. It becomes harder and harder to slay dragons if we are inviting them over for tea.

More than in the past, charted career paths will direct young women fresh out of college into the fold of conservation because of the explosion of opportunities in the next decade. Many heroines will arrive on the scene who are already waiting in the wings but have not yet positioned themselves as leaders. Many will leap from the ivory towers of academia into more active roles.

Inspirational leadership, though desperately needed, will be in shorter supply than managerial and technical leadership. In part this is a result of becoming more and more isolated from nature through an increasingly urbanized life-style. The toll of losing touch with our very sources of sustenance is the loss of passion for the planet. Yet we will act, more out of fear of consequence than from love for our Earth.

Women have the opportunity to be the quicksilver of the conservation movement as both free-lance warriors and trimtabs and captains of major ships. Their presence as leaders is more urgently needed than ever before. This is no secret alchemist's formula, only a balanced mixture of male and female. Men must recognize the need for loosening their lordly grip in order to right the balance, and women must demonstrate marked courage and daring in accepting the challenge.

Collectively, women have to *see* themselves as heroines of America's and the world's conservation and environmental movements in order to *be* heroines. As Jonathan Livingston Seagull said when he was learning how to fly through walls, "You can't go anywhere unless you first imagine yourself there!"

References

Colaw, Verda. 1983. "Putting Yourself in the Limelight." *Women in Forestry* 5, no. 3 (Fall).

Crum, Thomas F. 1987. *Magic of Conflict.* New York: Simon and Schuster.

Force, Jo Ellen. 1983–84. "Gender and Natural Resources: Is There a Relationship?" *Women in Forestry* 6, no. 1 (Winter).

Fox, Stephen. 1981. *John Muir and His Legacy: The American Conservation Movement*. Boston: Little, Brown.

Gilligan, Carol. 1982. *In a Different Voice*. Cambridge, Mass.: Harvard University Press.

Hepp, Donna. 1986. "Transitions: Gaining Experience for Management and Executive Positions." *Women in Forestry* 8, no. 1 (Spring).

James, Jennifer. 1983. "Changing Sex Roles and Adaptive Strategies." *Women in Forestry* 5, no. 1 (Spring).

Kellert, Stephen R., and Joyce K. Berry. 1987. "Attitudes, Knowledge and Behaviors Toward Wildlife as Affected by Gender." *Wildlife Society Bulletin* 15, no. 3 (Fall).

Kelly, Joyce M. 1986. "Women—Agents of Change." *Women in Forestry* 8, no. 1 (Spring).

Marburg, Sandra Lin. 1984. "Women and Environment: Subsistence Paradigms." *Environmental Review* 8 (Spring).

Merchant, Carolyn. 1984. "Women of the Progressive Conservation Movement: 1900–1916." *Environmental Review* 8 (Spring).

Norwood, Vera L. 1984. "Heroines of Nature: Four Women Respond to American Landscape." *Environmental Review* 8, no. 1 (Spring).

Thurber, Marshall, and Ron Kaufman. 1987. "Successful Leadership." *Windstar Journal* (Summer).

Wild, Peter. 1979. *Pioneer Conservationists of Western America*. Missoula, Mont.: Mountain Press Publishing.

Zieroth, Elaine J. 1988. "The Benefits of an Active Federal Women's Program." *Women in Natural Resources* 9, no. 3.

6 International Conservation Leadership and the Challenges of the Nineties

ALDEMARO ROMERO
*Executive Director and Chief Executive Officer, BIOMA,
Caracas, Venezuela*

ONE OF THE most important developments in the international conservation movement has been the flourishing of effective local organizations, particularly in Latin America, during the eighties. The nineties, however, present new challenges that will require many changes, not only in the way we conduct conservation tasks, but also in the relationships between the local groups and their U.S. counterparts.

Until the late 1970s there were very few organizations in the United States that put any effort into what is now called "international conservation." The recognition that most of the world's biodiversity is found in tropical nations and that many of the species of birds familiar to the United States are migrant ones that need safe places to live in Central and South America promoted the concept to "think globally, act locally" in the early 1980s. As a result, U.S. organizations have either helped to create new organizations in Latin America or supported existing ones. Since then, some of those local organizations have become quite successful despite the difficulties in developing new nonprofit institutions in countries with little tradition for private environmental action and philanthropic support.

This chapter will deal with what I believe are the key issues in the relationships between U.S. conservation organizations and their Latin American counterparts—issues that should be resolved rapidly and effectively if we really want to preserve in perpetuity a sizable representation of the world's natural heritage. These issues can be grouped into five categories: cultural barriers, training, science, ethics, and leadership. Although the different areas overlap in many instances, I have chosen them for the sake of organizing this discussion.

Cultural Barriers

Enormous cultural barriers separate U.S. and Latin American conservation organizations. These barriers present the most sensitive and complicated problems regarding the establishment of trust among the organizations. Most of us tend to ignore them, but this in turn causes a permanent sense of tension. Above all, we must remember that despite being in the same hemisphere, the United States does not share much history in common with countries south of the Rio Grande. Spanish America was first conquered and then colonized under the signs of the Inquisition and the Counter-Reformation, while Anglo-Saxons escaped from religious intolerance to the New World. While the United States based its independence on the liberal philosophy of John Locke, the French Revolution influenced the notion of independence in Latin America. These historical differences must be appreciated when comparing how conservationists from the United States and Latin America envision the environmental problems of the tropics.

For example, the destruction of the New World's rain forests is now a matter of fashion and newsworthiness in the developed world. While a few years ago the destruction of wetlands (and before that, during the height of Cousteau's popularity, the destruction of the oceans' resources) occupied such attention, today there is a sudden concern for the protection of rain forests. This faddishness may raise the awareness of the uninformed general public, but we in Latin America view all of these trends as inconsistent with real needs. Neither the oceans nor the wetlands were saved through faddish attention, nor, we suspect, will the rain forests be saved this way either.

We watch sadly as those sources of funding that yesterday supported wetlands conservation today support only the preservation of rain forests. Although we recognize the news value of stories about the rain forests for the American news media, we believe they have little impact on the conscience and attitudes of Latins.

In the same way, the "hamburger debate," which tried to reduce the complexities of forest preservation to the amount of fast food consumed by the American public, was viewed as specious in Latin America. Why? Because people in the United States generally do not perceive the pressures felt by many tropical countries to develop their pristine areas. Nor do North Americans comprehend how little moral authority is given to the natural resource experts in a country that bases its own development entirely on the rapid destruction of natural areas.

People and organizations on both sides of the Rio Grande have lacked the sensitivity and understanding necessary to provide effective solutions to the destruction of tropical rain forests. From the North we have seen generalized approaches to the problem, as if all Latin American countries were identical, as if experience in the United States could be transplanted anywhere, as if there were nothing worthwhile already in place in those countries, as if we had time to spend developing philosophies and planning endlessly without real interest in the objectives, and as if Latin American organizations should behave like local chapters of organizations in the United States.[1]

On the other hand, many attitudes in Latin America have also undermined the ability to attain swift and positive results. Latin Americans fail to understand that philanthropy as it is practiced north of the Rio Grande is almost unique to the United States, and that there are sincere reasons for doing something for the common good. At the other extreme we find some Latin groups willing to do anything their U.S. counterparts tell them to do as long as there is money available for it, even if it is a bad idea.

Conservation leaders in the United States need to communicate better with nongovernmental organizations (NGOs) in Latin America. New policies of communication should be based on the following principles:

1. Be candid about the nature of the relationship by clearly stating what is being offered and what is expected in return.
2. Maintain, through electronic and conventional mail as well as face-to-face meetings, a continuous flow of substantive information about the activities, challenges, successes, and difficulties of all cooperating organizations in the United States and Latin America.
3. Develop close relationships among the major sources of funding in the United States and the ultimate recipients of that support in Latin America, even if such an approach generates a shortsighted panic among the institutions based in the United States.

Only through effective and energetic communication will we be able to lower the cultural barriers that separate us. For historical, political and economic reasons, such initiatives must be advanced by U.S. organizations. There is more and more resentment in Latin America toward conservation organizations in the United States. U.S. groups have become increasingly less enthusiastic, generous, and committed than before, due in part to the fact that they have overextended themselves. Moreover, they have become less aggressive in pursuing hard cash and more entangled in "fund-raising" sideshows, such as debt swaps and cooperation with multilateral agencies. These actions look good to the shortsighted, but they do not meet Latin American needs for hard currency and a commitment in perpetuity.

Let both sides explore the problems that unite rather than divide them. For the first time, let both sides formulate serious and precise plans of action aimed at preserving most of what is left of the rain forests. But let us do it now, with the utmost frankness and determination, and not from the shadows of equivocal attitudes and misleading behavior.

Training

How do we provide sufficient training to the future *leaders* in conservation in developing countries? I must stress the word *leaders* since it is the key to the whole issue. We must remember that what we really need for the job are not simply managers but leaders—people who are able to provide a vision for the future. We need honest and creative men and women who possess a single-minded obsession for what they want to achieve, and the ability to communicate and motivate so that they receive the support they need.

We cannot create leaders; we may train them for specific tasks and offer them opportunities to improve and perfect themselves, but we cannot instill in them the attributes of leadership. Thus, the first task of any U.S. conservation group that wants to find an effective partner is to identify those people with leadership potential. I am sorry to say that there is no magic test for that, except that leaders always manage to distinguish themselves once challenges and opportunities are offered to them. What is required is the sensitivity to perceive leaders when they arise.

We thus cannot plan for a one-dimensional training program or a rigid academic curriculum. Some leaders will learn best through informal contacts with colleagues, by visiting new centers for the development of ideas, or by merely having access to information. Others will profit more from a scholastic approach. What is most important is that we learn to recognize leaders as they emerge.

In the 1970s and early 1980s, there were hardly any places in Latin America where regional conservation leaders could go for training. Peregrination to the United States to "learn the business" was almost an obligation. But things are changing. Now there are several successful Latin American organizations with one unquestionable advantage over their counterparts in the United States: They have saved land directly in the neotropics.

The time will come when Latin American conservation leaders will be trained at home and mostly by other Latins, so that they find experiences to which they can relate more easily. Such centers for learning, if properly designed for leaders, should resemble Plato's

Akademeia or Aristotle's *Lykeion*. They should be centers for both holistic and specialized approaches toward the science and art of conservation leadership and management—centers where ideas flow freely; places where every man and woman will learn according to individual requirements; places for strengthening strengths and weakening weaknesses, using the most modern communications techniques and stimulating the exchange of scholars, experts, and leaders; places where the future can be envisioned and its path can be mapped.

This may sound elitist to some, but I think it is realistic. The big changes in the course of human history have occurred thanks to an elite corps of leaders who knew what they had to do and how to do it, and, most important, who did it.

We will return to the topic of international leadership later.

Science

Continuous change and the revision of ideas and methods are the hallmarks of science. Yet many visiting scientists involved in tropical conservation seem to believe that the customs and practices they bring with them are immutable. A brief review will help to illustrate this problem.

From the earliest days of involvement of U.S. conservation groups in the neotropics, science programs have been sold as an indispensable tool for creating capabilities to identify, select, protect, and monitor natural areas.[2] Two different kinds of programs have been used, and both have strengths and weaknesses. The first one, which I will call the academic-random program, supports purely academic projects aimed at producing knowledge for its own sake. An example would be a study to determine how many eggs an endangered species lays. The program had its origin in the British perspective of wildlife conservation in Africa, where the units of conservation are the species, and the closer those species could be shown to be conservation "pets" the better.

This program may produce valuable information on species whose natural histories are unknown, thus allowing conservationists to have a better understanding of what they are trying to preserve. But since the researchers in charge of the program are intent upon producing results that will fit the standards of a thesis or a professional journal, these investigations produce a lot of information that could be considered "noise" for those who need specific facts in order to proceed with conservation management plans to protect natural areas rather than species. Also, this kind of program can cover, at best, only a handful of the species inhabiting high-diversity ecosystems such as coral reefs or tropical rain forests, and it rarely takes into account the problems of land management. Thus it can be termed both an academic and a random program.

The second program, which I call the typological program, involves the development of checklist-oriented inventories of fauna, flora, and ecosystems using cookbook methodologies and typologies. It was developed by U.S. scientists mostly to identify, select, and monitor the last remaining pockets of natural diversity in countries such as the United States, where most of the biological diversity had been wiped out by the turn of the century. In the United States, the big natural areas fell into the hands of park managers and the smaller, pocket areas became the responsibility of state governments and private conservation groups.

The typological program was thus engineered as an inventory-oriented task, identifying rare and threatened biota and using computers to record them. It was devised in part to influence state and local goverments to act whenever private conservation groups decided not to preserve pocket areas through acquisition, donation, leasing, or some form of cooperative agreement with private owners.

This kind of program is better suited to the identification, selection, design, and monitoring of small natural areas, since the information generated rapidly becomes *asymptotic*. It usually considers the same amount of information about terrestrial vertebrates and vascular plants, following a rigid methodology in order to ensure homogenous results. In this way it resembles the classification system proposed by numerical taxonomists in the 1960s.[3]

The typological program has been very successful in the United

States precisely because it works well in small areas with low bio-diversity. But when transplanted to the neotropics, the flaws in the program begin to appear.

First, we are dealing here with tropical lands of enormous bio-diversity. Moreover, the acreages proposed for national parks are substantial, often exceeding 1 million acres. These are not the tiny, low-diversity woodlots typically held by private conservation groups in the United States. Some of them rank in the top ten globally among areas identified for their biological diversity.

Second, the typologies developed for natural areas in the United States do not apply in the neotropics, where more complex but poorly known ecosystems abound. This forces the architects of the program to face one of the great dilemmas of the typological mind: whether to change the nomenclature and sometimes even the very nature of the "types," which are the very units of the research program.

Third, because of the vast acreages to be covered, one zoologist, one botanist, and one ecologist cannot possibly survey and categorize the biodiversity within a reasonable time, especially when there is an urgent need to protect the area. This has forced typologists to use remote sensing and geographic information systems, but these techniques do not come without resistance. They force profound changes in the ways in which typologists have operated successful programs in the United States. Resistance toward innovation is one of the great paradoxes of the scientific revolution as it is described by Thomas Kuhn.[4]

Conservation scientists in the neotropics do not suggest that typological programs should be abandoned, but that they should be modified and expanded to take into account the unprecedented scientific problems presented by tropical environments. This suggestion apparently sounds like heresy to the old-guard typologists of the U.S. conservation groups.

Another factor which cannot be ignored is that the economic survival of these programs in Latin America depends on how they are viewed with respect to solving local problems. For better or worse, Landsat photography and colorful maps tend to appear more useful to Latin American leaders than gray, Latinate lists of "elements of occurrence."

Moreover, information systems should be designed to include the characterization of human activities *within* the natural areas slated for preservation as well as in the surrounding areas. Fences and No Trespassing signs are hardly a source of local conflict in the United States, but in many parts of Latin America they are a prescription for trouble.

In order to make typological programs universal and effective in Latin America, we must

1. make them more flexible and maintain a philosophy of flexibility.
2. bring Latin American conservation scientists into the discussion so that the methodology becomes as useful as possible.
3. agree not to promote the methodology in Latin America as if it were a franchise, but rather make sure that each information system accommodates not only local ecological differences but also local needs.
4. agree to transfer new technologies to the information system centers in Latin America.

Ethics

Since the early 1980s, Latin American conservation groups have flourished in a difficult environment. They have managed not only to survive, but to accomplish tasks with undeniable technical skill. They once needed both technical and financial support from their counterparts in the United States, but their technical needs are now far fewer and their fund-raising capabilities, particularly at the local level, have improved. Nevertheless, they remain very much dependent on money raised from sources in the United States.

Meanwhile, conservation groups in the United States have also experienced an evolution. Financially, they are now much less supportive of Latin American organizations. I believe that this is the result of three problems: the overextension of programs, the lack of aggressiveness in opening new markets for international conservation within the philanthropic community of the United States, and a lack of courage and direction among the leadership of many organizations.

As a consequence, I see two trends that I believe are ethically questionable. One concerns the third-party management of money. The other relates to the way in which U.S.-based conservation groups choose how, when, and whom they should help.

With Latin American conservation groups becoming technically more proficient and gaining more direct access to important funders in the United States, the original role of international conservationists from the States has fallen into a twilight. Yet instead of reshaping themselves and injecting new vitality into their role as catalyzers promoting the maturity of Latin NGOs, many groups in the United States have proposed charging fees to cover the costs of fund-raising for Latin groups.

This new trend is dangerous because it converts what should be a purely philanthropic endeavor into a commercial one, thus altering the character of the relationship from a fight for a cause into a lucrative transaction. At its worst, this could frighten away good-faith donors who want to see all of their contribution go directly to the cause. We cannot afford to reduce the already tiny philanthropic market for international conservation.

When faced with these objections, the leaders of U.S. organizations respond that fund-raising carries a cost and that, after all, they do the same with their state chapters. But Latin American conservation groups should not be treated as chapters. They are and must continue to be independent. Moreover, the Latin groups remain fragile financially. Fees charged for transactions are dollars that are not spent where they are most needed. Latin American organizations would prefer working with fund-raising agents who share their mission of helping to preserve the world's natural heritage. There are legitimate for-profit groups that could raise money for a fee, but working with them smacks of commercializing our cause.

The other ethical issue concerns the direction in which the money should go. Since the beginning of relations among Latin and U.S.-based conservation groups, there has been much confusion on this point.

The tendency to try to do everything everywhere has stretched financial and personnel resources beyond manageability. The lesson from successful corporations that success depends on doing a few things well seems to have been ignored by many NGOs in the United States.

Once a diverse menu of countries, local NGOs, and projects has been established, the nightmare of questions begins. Should efforts be concentrated in countries where the ecological situation is the worst but the chances for success are dim? Should resources flow to local NGOs that have already shown vigor and the elements of success, or would they be better spent on groups that have never seemed to take off?

These are not easy choices to make, but I can help by harking back to my own original reason for getting involved in conservation: namely, to save what really can be saved as soon as possible. For that purpose, time, effort, and money are best spent where the chances of success are greatest. The cause is too important and the resources too limited to risk failure. No matter how much we desire to, we cannot save the whole world.

While many organizations in the United States have faced this reality, they have not always made the best choices. More and more emphasis is being placed on efforts that appear to be charitable and receive favorable press—the efforts in October 1988 to save three gray whales near Alaska, for example—but that have dubious merit in saving a species or a natural area. It is also of doubtful honor to help only those organizations that unerringly do as they are told.

Quality results will come from a relationship with quality partners who will necessarily be critical and independent. A clear message to follow rather than lead will discourage the good work and intentions of the well-staffed Latin American groups. They will not conduct themselves well with a banana republic mentality.

These are trends of deteriorating ethics. If they continue, we shall be faced with the subversion of the conservation cause and the corruption of the Latin groups. If organizations in the United States, born into a society of puritanical traditions, cannot hold true to their own principles, then what can be expected of organizations that work in an environment where the boundaries between what is legal and what is ethical are so much less clearly drawn?

It is time to respond to the challenges of a changing world creatively and honestly and, most important, in a way that will make us feel proud.

Leadership

The crisis we face in the relationships among our organizations is a crisis of leadership.

In the early 1980s, conservation groups in the United States promoted the idea of preserving the world's natural heritage through the actions of local organizations. They fully supported them with technical and financial aid, and in doing so the leadership of those groups in the United States demonstrated courage and vision. Without that, private action in international conservation would be much less promising and effective than it is today.

But today we face new challenges. The needs of organizations now in place are different than they were five or ten years ago. The continuing devastation of Latin American resources, the existence of new technologies that could be applied to conservation, the complexities and intricacies of each Latin American country, and the need for greater financial resources all cry out for more sophisticated leadership on both sides of the Rio Grande.

Our concern should be about the future. The old era is ending, and the old ways will no longer do. As Winston Churchill said: "If we open a quarrel between the present and the past, we shall be in danger of losing the future." Today we need a leadership that is more attentive to the agendas of the Latin groups than to the old political quarrels among organizations in the United States. We need a leadership that is more interested in making substantial contributions, which will lie far beyond the flashy debt-swap deals and the complicated schemes for solving problems with intricate, theoretical drawings. They lack realism. John F. Kennedy said: "Courage, not complacency, is our need today—leadership, not salesmanship."[5]

We cannot expect change to happen by itself. It is the responsibility of the leadership of the Latin American conservation movement to be persistent and patient—persistent in our determination to make our fellow conservationists in the North more aware and sensitive, patient against our desperation to see our problems solved as demanded by the circumstances.

I want to return now to the first proposal made in this chapter, for a meeting of the minds and spirits of the leadership of the two cultures. I remember how the chairman of a major organization in the United States told me, out of sincerity, that one of the biggest problems he faced in the international arena was that his organization did not know where to turn, where best to place resources in the arena of international conservation. My response could not have been more simple: Listen to us, listen to the ones who face the daily hardships of maintaining private organizations where there is little tradition for private action, who have to raise money where there is little tradition for philanthropy, who have to authorize the payroll with no guarantee that they will be able to do so again next year or even next month.

The 1990s will demand imagination, decisiveness, and courage. We face the choice between greatness or decline in our own organizations, between the fresh air of progress and the stale, dank atmosphere of the status quo. We face the choice between excellence and mediocrity. There are many who wait upon our decision.

Notes

1. For a more extensive discussion of these issues, see Aldemaro Romero, "Thirteen Fatal Errors," *Foundation News* 29 (4): 58–60.
2. I use the term "science program" in the same sense as D. L. Hull, *Science as a Process: An Evolutionary Account of the Social and Conceptual Development of Science* (Chicago: University of Chicago Press, 1988).
3. Hull, *Science as a Process.*

4. Thomas Kuhn, *The Structure of Scientific Revolutions* (Chicago: University of Chicago Press, 1970).

5. Acceptance of presidential nomination, Democratic National Convention, Los Angeles, California, July 15, 1960.

7 Science and the Conservation Leader

DANIEL SIMBERLOFF
Department of Biological Sciences, Florida State University

ANY EXECUTIVE OF an organization addressing scientific issues is faced with the problem of knowing enough of the science to form sound judgments and to speak with authority. Thus, the head of an essentially political organization militating for or against the Strategic Defense Initiative ("Star Wars") would not be credible without some grasp of the science and technology underlying the proposals. In particular, where there is debate about the efficacy of a course of action (as for Star Wars), an effective leader must be able to understand the issues well enough to do more than just add up the number of scientists on one side and the number on the other. Yet the person leading a conservation organization is not likely to be a scientist, and the scientific issues may be complex indeed. For Star Wars, the issues revolve around new technologies such as lasers and supercomputers as well as established sciences such as physics and mechanics.

A conservation leader confronts a situation at least as forbidding as Star Wars. First, conservation and environmental science comprise an amazingly broad set of scientific concerns, ranging from meteorology and global resource dynamics through genetic and demographic change in small populations to projected evolutionary patterns of the next few millennia. Second, the underlying sciences are, for the most part, quite young. The first American textbook in ecology was published in 1900 (Simberloff 1980); meteorology is a notoriously unpredictive science; and scientists are currently debating the form and relative importance of genetic and demographic changes in small populations.

Given the broad, fluid, and contentious nature of the relevant sciences, how can a conservation leader become sufficiently expert to be credible and to make correct decisions? Must one have a Ph.D. in the allied sciences? A large scientific staff? Where can one seek advice? Will some standard short course suffice? How should a conservation leader integrate available scientific information into his or her decisions?

Three courses of action will adapt conservation leaders to the scientific demands of their jobs. First, a series of readings in key areas (outlined below) will provide the necessary background. Second, a conservation leader must develop a network of expert advisors for advice on specific areas. This network must be large enough that the leader is never restricted to one trusted source of advice on an issue. Third, with the advice of the advisors, a conservation leader must remain abreast of relevant scientific developments through reading and conversation.

The first requisite would pertain to the leader of any organization, but the second and the third perhaps require elaboration. They derive from the breadth, relative novelty, and contentiousness of sciences that pertain to conservation. The following sections will detail the short history of conservation science. In an outline of necessary background for the leader of an organization concerned with Star Wars, one would not likely detail the history of physics. But for conservation, the details of its history are directly relevant because the fields are so new that even the earliest concepts are from the twentieth century and are more or less useful (and frequently applied) today. Further, in certain areas consensus changes so rapidly that conventional wisdom in one year would be viewed as dated the next year. However, it is a commonplace in the sociology and history of science that individual scientists may be more or less attached to particular ideas even after the field has developed beyond them. Thus, for any particular topic a conservation leader must have access to advice from several sources, and must have an extensive enough background and sound enough judgment to form sober opinions if the advice is conflicting. Further, the conservation leader must maintain an adequate background in the face of evolving sciences and technologies to aid in reaching these opinions. To some extent judgment will necessarily be judgment of persons: Which individual have given past advice that has proven sound? With which individuals has the leader been able to establish a trusting relationship? In other words, the nebulous area of "personal chemistry" will have a role, as it would in any organization. But interactions of personal chemistry are best catalyzed by accurate underlying knowledge.

The Status of Conservation Science

A corpus of scientific literature certainly exists for virtually any conservation issue. However, various parts of the literature reflect varying levels of underlying scientific maturity. One classification of the key sciences would be in order of increasing breadth of focus (and decreasing detail): (1) population biology, (2) community biology, (3) ecosystem processes, and (4) regional and global processes. Because the introduction of new species and the application of various restoration technologies can affect conservation at least at the first three levels, I will discuss these problems separately.

The biological sciences have most recently become the focus of attention of conservationists. Conversely, beginning in the mid-1970s, many biologists were newly attracted to conservation concerns. There were several reasons. First, the building perception of an environmental crisis, exemplified by Earth Day 1970, sensitized biologists as it did the lay public, and those who taught ecology and environmental science courses could hardly fail to become engaged. The first warning of a potential mass extinction in the tropics was in the 1970s (Raven 1976), as were articulate warnings about loss of biological diversity (e.g., Myers 1979). Furthermore, two new applications of current biological theory to conservation generated excitement: Island biogeographic theory was applied to refuge design (e.g., Goeden 1979; Temple 1981), and genetic theory was applied to the problem of extinction among small populations (e.g., Franklin 1980; Soulé 1980). This excitement and activity led directly to the formation in 1986 of a large professional organization, the Society for

Conservation Biology, and the initiation of its journal, *Conservation Biology*.

The trajectory described in the last paragraph, however, does not fully explain the introduction of biology into conservation. For example, from the late nineteenth century in the United States, scientists have been providing data and ideas on conservation that are reflected in the National Park System and many other federal and state refuges. At first this research was survey work—determining which species are found where and in what habitats. An underlying assumption was that protection of a species or community would simply require determining its ideal habitat and setting aside some of that habitat. Thus, refuges were established for particular species, such as the California condor, saguaro cactus, Joshua tree, and Kirtland's warbler. By the 1930s came a recognition that habitat could not just be set aside but also sometimes had to be maintained by active intervention, such as the use of fire to maintain some species and communities. This recognition was not without controversy in administrative circles (e.g., Schiff 1962), but scientists at least agreed on the principle, if not on the specifics, of such active stewardship. However, research and ideas deriving from biological science in the first half of this century are generally not much cited in the recent literature. The older sort of research, focused very narrowly on habitat requirements of specific species and communities, continues today in fields viewed by many biologists as slightly peripheral to "mainstream" biology: wildlife science and forestry. On the other hand, the wildlife science and forestry literatures have been loath to incorporate the "new" conservation biology.

The upshot is a rather disparate set of literatures. There are good compendiums of modern developments in wildlife science (e.g., Verner, Morrison, and Ralph 1986) and forestry (e.g., Jahn 1982) as well as collections of readings in the new conservation biology (e.g., Soulé 1986, 1987). Most of the former and at least half of the latter are accessible to the informed lay reader. Most useful for a conservation leader would be a single textbook for an upper-level college course that integrated the traditional and newer approaches to conservation and provided a critical overview of their strengths, limitations, and relationships. Unfortunately, the only such text currently is in Finnish (Järvinen and Miettinen 1987), with no immediate prospect of translation into English. It seems that the conservation leader must read three books rather than one. Even if there were a single text, a conservation leader would do well to seek advice from experts in three traditions—wildlife, forestry, and the new conservation biology.

Conservation biology is so new that, even though it has attracted an enormous amount of attention in both the professional and popular press (e.g., Gleick 1987; Wilford 1987) and deserves much credit for mobilizing a community of energetic and committed conservationists, its theories are untested. One must therefore view suggestions for specific courses of action with extreme caution. These suggestions generally fall into two areas primarily concerned with population biology—management of small populations and refuge design.

Population Biology

Small populations, even if well protected, are in danger of quick extinction, and recent attention has focused on three possible generic reasons (which are not mutually exclusive): demographic, environmental, and genetic (Shaffer 1981; Simberloff 1988). The demographic threat is that chance vicissitudes of birth and death could doom a population. For example, the probability that all individuals in one generation will happen to be of one sex increases as population size decreases. The environmental threat derives from random fluctuations in the physical environment. For example, a small population is likely to occupy a small geographic region, and would thus be more likely to be affected by a regional drought or a widespread fire. The short-term genetic threat comes from "inbreeding depression," the generally decreased fitness widely (but not universally) seen in inbred plants and animals. This problem is likely to be particularly acute in species that have traditionally not inbred but now are forced to do so, as in zoo animals or species that have recently suffered an abrupt decline and all reside in one or a few small, isolated populations. All within the space of about eight years (references in Simberloff 1988), attention first centered on the genetic threat as most important, then on the demographic threat, and most recently (e.g., Goodman 1987) a consensus may be building that the environmental threat is greatest.

My point in describing these developments is not to suggest that conservation leaders must have detailed knowledge of each of these threats or even an opinion on which is most important. Rather, leaders should have a general idea of what these threats are and the sorts of empirical phenomena ascribed to them. They should know that this is an area of active scientific work, both theoretical and empirical, so that published conclusions, especially concerning relative importance, are tentative. An organization would not want to commit all its resources, for example, to a technology to vitiate inbreeding depression (say, by moving animals or plants among refuges) without much more information than is currently available on just which species are likely to be threatened, and how much they are likely to be threatened, by genetic deterioration.

Franklin (1980) and others have described a longer-range genetic threat: As small populations inevitably lose genetic variability through "genetic drift" (the chance loss of genes because of the inherently random vagaries of gamete production and union), they may become so genetically depauperate that they will not be able to evolve in response to future environmental change. The underlying theoretical basis for this fear has recently been elucidated by Lande and Barrowclough (1987), but it is uncertain whether the assumptions of the theoretical model are realistic. In addition, there is an empirical lacuna because classical genetic experiments on response to selection have almost all been on fruit flies or highly inbred and previously selected farm animals (Simberloff 1988).

The recent literature on refuge design (e.g., Diamond 1975; Terborgh 1975; Wilson and Willis 1975) stems from the analogy comparing nature refuges to islands and consists primarily of attempting to apply the equilibrium theory of island biogeography (MacArthur and Wilson 1967). The key recommendations are:

1. Large refuges are preferable to small ones.
2. One large refuge is preferable to several small ones of equal total area.
3. Round refuges are preferable to elongated ones of equal area.
4. Corridors between refuges are desirable.

All four of these recommendations can be viewed as empirical propositions, and (except for the first) they differ strikingly from the traditional scientific approach to refuge selection: Determine the habitat requirements of species or communities of interest, then protect as much of that habitat as possible. Nevertheless, these recommendations are problematic; and, indeed, the general theory of island biogeography is questionable.

Whether these recommendations are valid in any particular instance depends greatly on the context. How large is "large," and how small is "small"? How expensive would the corridors be, and what is the probability that they might also transmit a contagious disaster like disease or fire? Most important, is the habitat in the alternative configurations really equal? Usually the answer to the latter question will be no, and the importance of even subtle differences in habitat is so well established (e.g., James et al. 1984) that one may have to weigh heavily even apparently minor differences. Even if different configurations would lead to different biotae if habitats were identical, the biotic differences might be quite hard to predict. For example, a number of authors have compared species lists for single large sites (or islands) with groups of small sites of equal total area and typically have found that groups of small sites contain more species (references in Simberloff 1988). However, this result is not automatically useful to refuge designers. For one thing, it might be that even if more species are found in the archipelago of small sites, certain species of particular conservation interest (for example, large vertebrates) might be found only in the large sites. For another, it might be that species diversity in the small sites will decay at a faster rate than in the large sites, so that several decades or centuries in the future the comparison would be very different. Unfortunately, the stakes in such an experiment would be very high, and the time span is clearly too long for refuge designers who must make decisions now.

Applications of island biogeographic theory to refuge design are of more than just academic interest, and because these ideas have reached even the lay press, administrators and decision makers are aware of them. There is a great danger that untested theory will be accepted uncritically, and the resultant errors will not always be on the side of conservatism. For example, Soulé, Wilcox, and Holtby (1979) announced that the largest East African savanna reserves were too small to sustain existing populations and were about to undergo a "faunal collapse" in which they would lose large fractions of their species within five millennia. This prediction was based not on observed extinctions, but rather on species-area relationships and hypothetical decay models. Boecklen and Gotelli (1984) demonstrated that, in fact, the predictive power of the models was so low that the correct prediction would call for losses of between 0.2 percent and 100 percent of their species in 5,000 years. Similarly, Newmark (1987) claimed that even the largest national parks in the American West were too small and had already lost about a fourth of their mammals, a claim widely repeated in American newspapers (e.g., Gleick 1987). However, a detailed rebuttal (Quinn, Van Riper, and Salwasser 1988) contended that these conclusions were based on faulty data and that there had been virtually no extinctions of large mammals in these parks.

If an organization is faced with a decision about whether to aid in refuge design or maintenance, it is critical to understand whether or not the refuge is doomed to be insufficient. The underlying science in this issue is new, is tentative, and has not been subjected to extended examination and criticism, though press releases do not make this uncertainty clear. This is one situation where sound background plus trusted scientific advice is critical.

Community Ecology

In the early years of ecology, populations were not considered a proper focus of study (e.g., Shelford 1913), and attention turned to the "superorganismic" community—a holistic, highly integrated entity with all populations fitting together in a harmonious, organized whole. The roots of this idea of an inherent balance of nature lay among the pre-Socratic Greeks (Egerton 1973). Though there were occasional skeptics, early twentieth-century ecologists generally adopted the view of a balanced nature epitomized by a superorganismic community. The key work that set the stage for half a century of ecological research was the first American textbook on ecology, *Research Methods in Ecology,* by Frederic Clements (1905). Clements forcefully described plant communities as integrated superorganisms. This conception of nature became the dominant paradigm not only in America but in Europe as well (McIntosh 1980; Simberloff 1980), to the extent that observations of individual species' populations, independently of the community, were not viewed as acceptable scientific research; people adopting this "individualistic" view, such as H. A. Gleason, were ostracized (McIntosh 1975). This is a great pity for conservationists because the dominant paradigm precluded important data on which species were actually presented before changes wrought by humans. For example, Margaret B. Davis, a leading authority on long-term vegetation change, has argued: "We do not know what the virgin vegetation of the pioneer days was like because all the ecologists were so busy looking for a nonexistent climax [community] that they forgot to record what was actually growing there" (Colinvaux 1973).

The inevitable reaction came in 1947 (Simberloff 1980), when three respected plant ecologists independently published data-based papers in *Ecological Monographs* forcefully attacking the Clementsian paradigm. They all cited Gleason's individualistic conception of plant communities as the correct alternative. Subsequent research on plant communities along these lines (e.g., Curtis 1955; Whittaker 1956, 1967) led to the replacement of the superorganism, so that the new generation of ecology textbooks in the early 1970s (e.g., Krebs 1972;

Colinvaux 1973) all agreed that species frequently act independently of one another, or at most are coordinated into small groups rather than into all-encompassing, integrated communities. The superorganism is not quite dead. It crops up in the literature of popular environmentalism (e.g., Commoner 1971) and in theoretical community ecology (references in Simberloff 1980). But it is certainly seen as an archaic view of nature by most ecologists.

This is not to say that communities are nothing but the collection of species present in one place at one time. Recent field research has shown that though interactions for most species are restricted to a limited group of other species (Paine 1980), most communities involve subsets of species that interact in stylized ways, with two consequences: (1) Certain species cannot be maintained without other interacting species, and (2) a species may so heavily affect so many other species in a community that the community cannot remain as a recognizable entity without it.

There are many well-known examples of such interactions. Wire grass, longleaf pine, red-cockaded woodpeckers, and fire are intricately linked in southeastern forests. The endangered woodpecker nests in old, dying longleaf and loblolly pines, exactly the sort of trees that are being replaced throughout the Southeast with faster-growing pulpwood. Longleaf pine thrives only in association with a ground cover including wire grass, which facilitates fire. Fire, in turn, is required for longleaf germination and also eliminates hardwood competitors. But wire grass propagates largely by stolons, so it recolonizes very slowly once removed. In fact, cleared longleaf and wire grass areas often do not return to longleaf and wire grass when left unmanaged.

Frogs of the World Wildlife Fund's Minimum Critical Size of Ecosystems project in Brazil are equally instructive. Four species breed only in peccary wallows and other small permanent ponds. Conserving these frogs therefore depends on maintaining peccaries or mimicking their wallows (Zimmerman and Bierregaard 1986).

In these examples, an understanding of the habitat and the ecological interactions of the species yielded information necessary for its conservation. No matter what the refuge configuration and how

large the refuges, certain Amazon frogs will not survive without peccaries or a substitute for peccary activity. Without fire, the longleaf
community is doomed to extinction no matter the size and shape of
reserves. Each system is idiosyncratic and required intensive study,
but the apparent slow pace of such studies should not lead to pessi-
mism. Ecologists recognize that focusing on certain types of species
will allow more rapid progress than would randomly sampling the
world's biota.

For example, certain key species interact crucially with many others in some communities. These "keystone species" (Paine 1974) tend
to be either mutualists (such as pollinators) of species that contribute
most biomass to the community or else predators on strong competitors for space. In some instances they are species that maintain key
landscape features, such as peccaries, beavers, or reef-building corals.
Understanding the interactions of a keystone species facilitates its
conservation, along with the conservation of a significant part of the
entire community. For example, palm nuts and figs are keystones in
a Peruvian tropical forest (Terborgh 1986). Palm nuts escape from all
but a group of specialist species who either have powerful jaws or else
can gnaw the nuts. Thus, there are few consumers, but among them
are peccaries and capuchins comprising about 30 percent of the total
frugivore biomass. Figs are eaten by all large primates, procyonids,
marsupials, and many birds. The upshot is that only 12 of 2,000 plant
species maintain almost all frugivores for three months of the year.

From the wildlife literature comes the concept of the "indicator
species," a species whose fate indicates that of a substantial component of the community. Thus, monitoring a group of indicator species can substitute for monitoring the entire community. Although
the designation of an indicator species has generally been rather ad
hoc, modern statistical methods allow more objective methods of
choice. A good example of an indicator species is the northern spotted owl. The Forest Service is required to predict how its management practices will affect indicator species. The northern spotted owl
was selected as an indicator for old-growth forest in the Pacific
Northwest on the grounds that its conservation would automatically
entail conservation of populations of many other species, such as the

old-growth trees, northern goshawk, silver-haired bat, red tree vole, and northern flying squirrel. It is not that the owl interacts directly with all of these species (though the last two are major prey items); rather, the habitat requirements are so similar that it is possible to predict that enough prime habitat conserved to save the owl will also save the other species. Once the indicator species concept is understood, then managing a site specifically for the indicator (as suggested by several timber interests for the spotted owl), far from being a valid conservation approach, is a legalistic evasion of the underlying conservation rationale (Simberloff 1987).

Unfortunately, the study of the forces that bind species together into communities, and the fragility of those forces, is still a young and contentious field (Lewin 1983), and most of the literature is in highly academic terms that would not provide the sort of overview a conservation leader requires. This is yet another area in which a conservation leader will have to depend on a scientific staff or advisors to stay abreast of developments in the field and for a sense of the validity of various courses of action.

Ecosystem Processes

The integration of the physical environment with biotic communities to form a dynamic, holistic entity—the ecosystem—was a twentieth-century achievement (McIntosh 1980). The key empirical studies were those describing the flow of energy through the system by means of trophic interactions among the component populations (Elton 1927; Lindemann 1942). A second observation was that nutrients flow along with the energy. Nutrient cycles have abiotic components (weathering of rock, for example) as well as biotic ones, and it was inevitable that a focus on the flow of nutrients would entail not only communities but the physical environment in which they are embedded.

Development of the ecosystem concept, by virtue of the size and complexity of ecosystems, received impetus from the mathematical techniques of systems analysis, and these elements converged in the

1960s in the work of E. Odum, H. T. Odum, and R. Margalef (McIntosh 1980). The plethora of research initiated in the mid-1960s with the International Biological Program (IBP) has led to a number of empirical findings on the functioning of particular ecosystems and to a variety of theories, many of which are summarized by Johnson (1977).

Empirical research on ecosystems has demonstrated how ecosystem function can severely constrain conservation efforts and management techniques. For example, Amazonian rain forest, though extremely productive, grows on nutrient-poor soil (Jordan and Herrera 1981). The nutrients that drive the system are in the vegetation itself, rather than in the soil, and the community has many biological mechanisms, such as an absorptive root mat (Jordan 1982) and an extraordinary microorganismic and fungal component (Janos 1983), that prevent nutrients from leaching out of the system. Nutrient cycles are therefore much more biotically based and complex than in the average temperate forest ecosystem, and the maintenance of particular tropical forest tree species is impossible without maintenance of the associated mechanisms—the root mat, the mycorrhizal fungi, and so forth.

Focus on nutrient flow and energy cycling suggests techniques for refuge establishment and maintenance. For example, Jordan (1982) has shown that some tropical forests can be maintained in the face of limited harvesting as long as the harvested areas are arranged in narrow strips parallel to elevational contours. This configuration succeeds because it maintains the biological community that minimizes nutrient loss and prevents rainfall from causing unbearable leaching. There is also the promise that nutrient flow in many ecosystems can be managed even with the loss or depletion of particular key species if other species can be found (or genetically engineered) to serve the threatened function. For example, there is intensive current interest in genetically engineering plants to fix their own nitrogen, and such a development could lessen an entire ecosystem's dependence on particular nitrogen-fixing bacteria and mycorrhizal fungi.

Fortunately for the conservation leader, there are summaries of ecosystem structure and function in less technical terms than those describing community-level phenomena. Among several introductory textbooks in general ecology, Odum (1971) and Krebs (1985) have particularly concise and lucid expositions on ecosystems, while a number of environmental problems relating to ecosystem function are summarized in a recent report by the National Research Council (1986).

Regional and Global Processes

The last few years have seen heightened public concern about several regional or global problems: global warming, acid precipitation, depletion of atmospheric ozone, and ocean fouling. Public concern seems most focused on human health or economic matters, but there is increasing worry among scientists about the conservation consequences of various large-scale phenomena.

These regional and global phenomena share the attribute that they arise from the cumulative impact of many more or less limited and apparently rather innocuous insults to the environment. Many rest on processes of dispersal and concentration by physical media (particularly air and water), and sometimes by living organisms as well (for example, as animals migrate, they may carry a nutrient or a pollutant). In other words, many problems of cumulative impacts boil down to the mobilization of some chemical (carbon dioxide, acids, et cetera) from many different sources and its subsequent redistribution. Small wonder that this is a complex issue, entailing fluid and atmospheric dynamics, meteorology, and organic and inorganic chemistry. Also small wonder that it is very difficult to predict the effects of many cumulative impacts. Other cumulative impacts rest not on generation and redistribution of a chemical, but on proliferation of a process. For example, fragmentation—the increasing subdivision of various habitats into groups of smaller and smaller parcels—is widely viewed as the single greatest current conservation problem (Simberloff 1988). A single housing development of several thousand hectares that transforms continuous forest into a landscape of lawns, paved areas, and a few patches of forest of a hundred hectares each will often have minimal direct effect on any single species or community type. Cumulatively, a thousand projects of this sort can be devastating. Similarly, an individual whale hunt may not detectably increase the probability of extinction for a whale species, while a number of them each year can reduce the species to a precarious state.

All cumulative impacts share the feature that numerous small, relatively harmless decisions can combine to produce utter disaster. The outlines of how such disasters arise are briefly summarized by Odum (1982) and the U.S. National Research Council (1986), while the Canadian Environmental Assessment Research Council and the U.S. National Research Council (1986) concisely state the scientific specifics of particular problems engendered by cumulative impacts and project necessary future research. Fortunately, all three of these works can be grasped by a nonscientist; they should all be read by any conservation leader.

The conservation implications of global warming are so transcendent, and potentially so devastating, that conservation organizations must consider this threat in many of their current daily activities. We should reach global average temperatures by 2050 that are higher than at any time in the last 150,000 years. One can forecast with assurance that many wetlands will be submerged within a century; obviously, current refuge design must take this fact into account. With somewhat less assurance, one can predict great changes in rainfall patterns so that some moist areas will become dry and vice versa. The geographic ranges of many plant and animal species will shift greatly, as they did during the Pleistocene glaciations and interglacials. Ranges of tree species will shift hundreds of miles and can probably be predicted quite accurately because paleobotanists have already documented such shifts from the Pleistocene. Thus, a park south of Maine or Vermont could not contain sugar maples for very long. Again, such information must be brought to bear on current land acquisition and refuge design. No single nontechnical summary of global warming causes and effects is now available, but the proceedings of a recent symposium will soon remedy this situation (Peters 1989).

Acid rain, though not as universal a problem as global warming (and an easier problem to solve), has already had major regional impacts on both lakes and forests and should already be taken into account in many conservation programs. Many lakes have already lost species (particularly of fishes) while forests have been greatly and perhaps irreversibly damaged by acid deposition. For example, the eastern hardwood forest on the top of Mount Mitchell in North Carolina has been at least as devastated by acid deposition as have the forests of Yellowstone National Park in the recent fires. Natural reseeding on Mount Mitchell will be substantially less than at Yellowstone. At the least, forest composition of many eastern forests will be greatly changed as acid-tolerant species replace susceptible ones. Stewardship of forests and lakes subjected to acid precipitation will be an increasingly difficult task, and will require expensive technologies (such as titration) that are virtually unknown outside of academic laboratories.

Fortunately, the outlines of the acid precipitation problem and the current state of scientific understanding of its consequences are clearly given by the U.S. National Research Council (1983) and Kennedy (1988) in a form that is largely accessible to the educated lay reader. An excellent introduction to forest problems is by Postel (1984).

The problem of wastes in the ocean has been heralded at least since Rachel Carson published *Silent Spring* in 1962, but concern about the marine environment seems to have been crystallized recently more by closed beaches and garbage washing ashore than by years of scientific concern over dwindling populations of various marine species. The biodiversity of the oceans is possibly even more poorly known than that of tropical forests (Ray 1988), and conservationists have generally paid far less attention to marine problems than to terrestrial and freshwater ones. Nevertheless, marine processes affect many systems of conservation interest. For example, where a conservation effort is focused on an estuary or other marine wetland, degradation of marine waters can devastate a terrestrial community, as when oil fouls a marsh. Similarly, terrestrial animals that feed at sea—many species of birds, for example—can be greatly affected by ocean pollution, which can decimate their prey populations or, through "biological magnification" of a chemical pollutant, generate pathological or even lethal physiological states.

Among numerous research publications on marine pollution and its effects are two concise, nontechnical summaries by Patin (1982) and the Office of Technology Assessment (1987).

Introduced Species

As humans began to travel widely, they inevitably spread a number of plants and animals, both deliberately and inadvertently. The results of these biological invasions have often been devastating (Elton 1958; Crosby 1986). For example, many native island bird species have been eliminated or brought to the brink of extinction through predation on their nests by introduced predators or through avian diseases carried by resistant invaders. Predatory insects and snails deliberately introduced for the control of introduced pests have occasionally attacked and virtually eliminated nontarget native invertebrates (Howarth 1985). Introduced insects such as the gypsy moth and plant pathogens such as chestnut blight and Dutch elm disease have drastically modified eastern American forests and rendered formerly common species rare. In southern Florida, the Australian melaleuca tree is in the process of displacing native pond cypress from ecotones between pinelands and swamps by being even more tolerant of the wide range of moisture and fire regimes that typify this habitat (Myers 1984).

Direct effects of introduced species on particular native species fall under the rubric of population biology and are well known in the nontechnical literature (e.g., Elton 1958). Perhaps less well known are many effects of introduced species on entire communities or ecosystems. One way such drastic effects can arise is if the introduced organism happens to become a keystone species, as defined above: a species that interacts crucially with many others in the community. For example, the periwinkle, a European snail introduced into Nova Scotia 150 years ago and currently spreading southward, eats algae on rocks and the underground portions of marsh grasses. Without the snails, coastal rocks are quickly covered with algae and mud, entraining a successional process that turns the rocky beach into a marsh. Bertness (pers. comm.) feels that many rocky beaches as far south as New England were originally marshes. Alternatively, an introduced species can greatly reduce or eliminate a keystone species. Dutch elm disease and the beetle that transports it fall into this category.

A species can also affect the entire ecosystem into which it is introduced by changing energy flow or nutrient cycling. For example, salt cedars introduced to the American Southwest are deeply rooted and have high transpiration rates; once established, they can change water availability and therefore the entire native plant community. They have even been known to cause a large marsh to dry completely in about thirty years (Vitousek 1986). In both the Great Smoky Mountains and Hawaii, feral pigs from Europe change the soil in a variety of ways, including significantly increasing nitrogen availability (Vitousek 1986). Such a change almost certainly affects the species composition of the resident plant community even more drastically than does the direct herbivory and rooting by the pigs. Similarly, introduced nitrogen-fixing plants can greatly affect the resident plant community by modifying the nitrogen cycle. In Hawaii an Atlantic shrub, *Myrica faya,* recently invaded volcanic areas that are very poor in nitrogen, particularly young lava flows and ash deposits. There are no native nitrogen-fixers, and *Myrica* forms near monocultures in some of these regions (Vitousek 1986, 1988). Nitrogen fixation by *Myrica,* in turn, is likely both to alter primary succession and to facilitate the introduction of further exotics, many of which favor more nitrogen-rich sites.

Ecologists have recently become concerned that genetically engineered organisms released into the environment may have effects at levels ranging from the population through the ecosystem, by analogy to similar effects caused by introduced species (Regal 1986). Among potential projects are rendering plant populations resistant to insect pests and also, as noted above, giving plants greatly increased ability to fix nitrogen. These examples should demonstrate the basis for concern over such projects.

A spate of recent publications on introduced species makes it quite easy for a conservationist to understand the variety and general nature of threats from these species. Collections edited by Mooney and Drake (1986) and Drake (1988) contain largely nontechnical descriptions of myriad effects of introduced species at all levels.

Restoration Technologies

Inevitably, as more and more land is developed and as various sorts of pollution continue, conservation organizations will increasingly shift their attention from sequestering the dwindling number of remaining unprotected sites toward stewardship of those already "protected" and restoration of threatened species and damaged habitats. Earlier I noted the long-standing recognition of a need for active stewardship, even if the particular stewardship technologies have occasionally been controversial. Restoration ecology is a newer field. It has already been attempted at the population, community, and ecosystem levels; one hopes that regional and global problems will ultimately be attacked in a biosphere restoration project. For now, the more mundane lower-level technologies demand attention.

Reintroduction of species to parts of their ranges from which they have been extinguished is a venerable technique. Many of the bison roaming western American rangeland are derived from captive stock in the Bronx Zoo (Cade 1988). Several birds of prey have been successfully reestablished over wide areas (Cade 1988). Griffith et al. (1989) surveyed the vast and scattered literature and reported that birds and mammals were by far the most frequent targets of reintroduction attempts and that out of hundreds of projects, native game birds and mammals successfully reestablished populations in a majority of cases. But success for "threatened, endangered, and sensitive" species was certain in fewer than 15 percent of the attempts. Many reintroduction attempts include an expensive prerelease captive breeding program deploying elaborate technologies (e.g., Conway 1988; Dresser 1988; Seal 1988), but captive-bred animals are often ill-adapted for life in the wild for genetic, physiological, or behavioral reasons (Lyles and May 1986; Cade 1988). Therefore, though reintroduction projects often have great emotional appeal, a conservation leader must demand a hard-nosed scientific assessment before embarking on this course.

Community and ecosystem restoration is a newer field and is at least as expensive as species reintroductions. Although virtually any kind of reforestation project or successional process can be construed as restoration, in fact the reconstruction of a semblance of an original community, with ecosystem processes such as energy flow and nutrient cycling similar to their original condition, is a much more difficult problem in many environments. There is little precedent for such large-scale attempts as the reconstruction of dry tropical forest in Costa Rica (Janzen 1988) or old-growth mixed forest in Wisconsin (Luoma 1988). Even the exact nature of the original state is incompletely known; so such projects should be conceived as large, long-term experiments, and sufficient data should be gathered to assess their results. Monitoring of the required sort is an unfortunate rarity in environmentally questionable projects (National Research Council 1986). On a smaller scale, numerous wetlands and aquatic system restorations have been attempted (Cairns 1988; Zedler 1988) and monitored, with mixed results. For example, Zedler (1988) notes that there is as yet no evidence that an artificial tidal wetland can replace the functions of a natural one, and that assessments of wetland restoration have never encompassed the entire ecosystem, but only selected species.

Given the potential importance of reintroduction and restoration technologies and their expense, conservation leaders will have to familiarize themselves with the goals, prospects, and methods in this field. An excellent introduction is provided by a series of chapters in the recent volume edited by Wilson (1988). However, this is another science in which any particular proposal will demand specific scientific advice, and the scientists with expertise in this field are largely different from those with expertise in the fields already discussed.

Conclusion

In most areas concerning a conservation leader, a small number of basic readings will not make him or her an expert, but will provide sound information on the nature of the problem and current scientific thrusts to deal with it. These readings, outlined above, would constitute approximately two reading courses in graduate school and so would not be an unreasonable burden. As I noted in the beginning, a common thread running through many of the areas is that they are active foci for research, with few real consensuses and with rapidly changing views. Population and community biology certainly exemplify this contentious, labile nature. Although debates about ecosystem, regional, and global processes have not, by and large, been quite so contentious, one can point to disputes and unanswered questions at all levels. The very fact of a flurry of recent publishing activity on introduced species is proof of the unsettled nature of this field. Arguments about the potential ecological threats of genetically engineered organisms, and the relevancy of studies of introduced species for understanding these threats, have led to an extraordinary symposium of the American Society for Microbiology (Halvorson, Pramer, and Rogul 1985) and an even more extraordinary booklet by the U.S. National Academy of Sciences (1987) attempting to alleviate concerns but quite possibly having the opposite effect.

So a conservation leader, even one very familiar with the fundamental relevant issues, will often be forced to evaluate different potential courses of action in the absence of a very clear scientific mandate. Perhaps the most obvious example of this dilemma is refuge acquisition and design. It is thus imperative that a conservation leader have strong, multiple lines of communication with active scientists in the key disciplines. The nature of those lines will doubtless vary with the mission and scope of the organization as well as the personal management style of the leader, but it is inconceivable that even a well-read leader could formulate consistently appropriate policy and make consistently defensible decisions in a scientific vacuum. A large organization can have a scientific staff; a small one can have a more or less formal advisory panel. In either instance, a conservation leader should foster personal contacts to be exploited at times when a question has scientific content but scientific conventional wisdom is ambiguous. Granted that, on such questions, a conservation leader's scientific contacts may well not all give the same advice, gradually he or she will come to value and seek input from certain individuals more than from others, as does a leader in any field. In science perhaps even more than in other areas, an ongoing publication record in recognized, refereed journals should be proof of an advisor's credibility. On the other hand, absence of such a record would argue against continued reliance on someone who may give unsound advice.

Personal scientific contacts can aid a conservation leader in another necessary task. Above I have cited a few background readings for evaluating current conservation proposals. But the entire history of the field suggests that some of these areas will be seen as less important in the future, and certainly some new areas that I have not even touched on will receive attention. On the first Earth Day virtually no one discussed the genetic underpinnings of conservation problems. Nowadays genetics is one of the main concerns. At least as important as a particular set of background readings, then, are the recognition that there will always be new critical background readings and the ability to identify these. Scientists can help greatly both in pointing to the new areas and in acquiring background knowledge.

A network of formal and informal scientific contacts will also preadapt conservation leaders for a set of decisions that will become increasingly important and will involve the commitment of massive resources. These decisions will be on the extent to which conservation organizations should themselves conduct or commission research rather than take from the academic literature those concepts, techniques, and theories that seem relevant. To some extent such research is already sponsored by some conservation organizations, particularly in the areas of stewardship, biodiversity surveys, and information storage and retrieval. Nevertheless, by far the greatest share of scientific information marshaled by conservation organizations is still produced by government scientists or by university or institute scientists, who are often funded by grants from various government agencies. Though much of this information is valuable, inevitably the goals of conservation organizations will differ somewhat from those of academics and government agencies. This difference alone suggests that, at the very least, conservation organizations will wish to influence external research. They may even wish to conduct or fund research themselves, just as private industry does. In a climate where government support of academic research generally and ecological research in particular is inadequate and shrinking, it is even more likely that conservation organizations will have to turn inward for some of their scientific research.

Taking such a course of action will be expensive and, with respect to scientific advice, even more difficult than the other kinds of decisions a conservation leader may have to make. This is because scientists are even less likely to be dispassionate and "scientific" in judging the merits of their own research than they are in judging other research. This is the reason that federal grant-making panels operate under stringent conflict-of-interest laws. A conservation leader's scientific contacts should include persons with a direct interest in conservation research—this is one reason they are willing to serve in this capacity at all and one reason their advice is expert. However, as conservation organizations move toward direct support of research, such contacts will, at times, have more or less severe conflicts of interest. This problem makes it doubly important that a conservation leader have multiple lines of communication with the scientific community. In conservation as in industry, it is unwise to rely on a sole source.

References

Boecklen, W. J., and N. J. Gotelli. 1984. Island biogeographic theory and conservation practice: Species-area or specious-area relationship? *Biol. Conserv.* 29:63–80.

Cade, T. J. 1988. Using science and technology to reestablish species lost in nature. Pp. 279–88 in Wilson, 1988.

Cairns, J., Jr. 1988. Increasing diversity by restoring damaged ecosystems. Pp. 333–43 in Wilson, 1988.

Canadian Environmental Assessment Research Council and National Research Council (U.S.). 1986. *Cumulative environmental effects: A binational perspective.* Ottawa: C.E.A.R.C. and N.R.C.

Clements, F. E. 1905. *Research methods in ecology.* Lincoln, Nebr.: University Publ. Co.

Colinvaux, P. A. 1973. *Introduction to ecology.* New York: Wiley.

Commoner, B. 1971. *The closing circle.* New York: Knopf.

Conway, W. 1988. Can technology aid species preservation? Pp. 263–68 in Wilson, 1988.

Crosby, A. W. 1986. *Ecological imperialism: The biological expansion of Europe, 900–1900.* Cambridge: Cambridge Univ. Press.

Curtis, J. T. 1955. A prairie continuum in Wisconsin. *Ecology* 36:558–66.

Diamond, J. M. 1975. The island dilemma: Lessons of modern biogeographic studies for the design of natural reserves. *Biol. Conserv.* 7:129–46.

Drake, J. A., ed. 1988. *Biological invasions.* Chichester: Wiley.

Dresser, B. L. 1988. Cryobiology, embryo transfer, and artificial insemination in ex situ animal conservation programs. Pp. 296–308 in Wilson, 1988.

Egerton, F. N. 1973. Changing concepts of the balance of nature. *Quart. Rev. Biol.* 48:322–50.

Elton, C. 1927. *Animal ecology.* New York: Macmillan.

———. 1958. *The ecology of invasions by animals and plants.* London: Methuen.

Franklin, I. R. 1980. Evolutionary change in small populations. Pp. 135–50 in M. E. Soulé and B. A. Wilcox, eds., *Conservation biology: An evolutionary-ecological perspective.* Sunderland, Mass.: Sinauer.

Gilbert, F. S. 1980. The equilibrium theory of island biogeography: Fact or fiction? *J. Biogeogr.* 7:209–35.

Gleick, J. L. 1987. Species vanishing from many parks. *New York Times,* Feb. 3, p. 15, 17.

Goeden, G. B. 1979. Biogeographic theory as a management tool. *Environ. Conserv.* 6:27–32.

Goodman, D. 1987. The demography of chance extinction. Pp. 11–34 in Soulé, 1987.

Griffith, B., J. M. Scott, J. W. Carpenter, and C. Reed. 1989. Translocation and reintroduction as species conservation tools: Results of a survey. Ms. subm.

Halvorson, H. O., D. Pramer, and M. Rogul, eds. 1985. *Engineered organisms in the environment: Scientific issues.* Washington, D.C.: American Society for Microbiology.

Howarth, F. G. 1985. Impact of alien land arthropods and mollusks on native plants and animals in Hawaii. Pp. 149–79 in Stone, C. P., and J. M. Scott, eds., *Hawaii's terrestrial ecosystems: Preservation and management.* Proceedings of symposium, June 5–6, 1984, Hawaii Volcanoes National Park. Honolulu: Coop. National Park Res. Studies Unit, Univ. of Hawaii.

Jahn, G., ed. 1982. *Handbook of vegetation science, Part XIII: Application of vegetation science to forestry.* The Hague: W. Junk.

James, F. C., R. F. Johnston, N. O. Wamer, G. J. Niemi, and W. J. Boecklen. 1984. The Grinnellian niche of the wood thrush. *Amer. Natur.* 124:17–30.

Janos, D. P. 1983. Tropical mycorrhizas, nutrient cycles, and plant growth. Pp. 327–45 in Sutton, S. L., T. C. Whitmore, and A. C. Chadwick, eds., *Tropical rain forests: Ecology and management.* Oxford: Blackwell.

Janzen, D. H. 1988. Tropical dry forests: The most endangered major tropical ecosystem. Pp. 130–37 in Wilson, 1988.

Järvinen, O., and K. Miettinen. 1987. *Sammuuko suuri suku?* Helsinki: Suomen Luonnonsuojelun Tuki Oy.

Johnson, P. L. 1977. *An ecosystem paradigm for ecology.* Oak Ridge, Tenn.: Oak Ridge Associated Universities.

Jordan, C. F. 1982. Rich forest, poor soil. *Garden* 6(1):11–16.

Jordan, C. F., and R. Herrera. 1981. Tropical rain forests: Are nutrients really critical? *Amer. Natur.* 117:167–80.

Kennedy, I. R. 1988. *Acid soil and acid rain.* Research Studies Press.

Krebs, C. J. 1972. *Ecology: The experimental analysis of distribution and abundance.* New York: Harper & Row.

———. 1985. *Ecology: The experimental analysis of distribution and abundance,* 3rd ed. New York: Harper & Row.

Lande, R., and G. F. Barrowclough. 1987. Effective population size, genetic variation, and their use in population management. Pp. 87–123 in Soulé, 1987.

Lewin, R. 1983. Santa Rosalia was a goat. *Science* 221:636–39.

Lindemann, R. L. 1942. The trophic-dynamic aspect of ecology. *Ecology* 23:399–418.

Luoma, J. R. 1988. In Wisconsin, a debate over ways to manage national forest growth. *New York Times,* Oct. 18, p. 22.

Lyles, A. M., and R. M. May. 1986. Problems in leaving the ark. *Nature* 326:245–46.

MacArthur, R. H., and E. O. Wilson. 1967. *The theory of island biogeography.* Princeton: N.J.: Princeton Univ. Press.

McIntosh, R. P. 1975. H. A. Gleason—"Individualistic ecologist" 1882–1975: His contributions to ecological theory. *Bull. Torry Bot. Club* 102:253–73.

———. 1980. The background and some current problems of theoretical ecology. *Synthese* 43:195–255.

Mooney, H. A., and J. A. Drake, eds. 1986. *Ecology of biological invasions of North America and Hawaii.* New York: Springer-Verlag.

Myers, N. 1979. *The sinking ark: A new look at the problem of disappearing species.* Oxford: Pergamon Press.

Myers, R. L. 1984. Ecological compression of *Taxodium distichum var. nutans* by *Melaleuca quinquenervia* in Southern Florida. Pp. 358–64 in Ewel,

K. C., and H. T. Odum, eds., *Cypress Swamps*. Gainesville, Fla.: Univ. of Florida Press.

National Academy of Sciences (U.S.). 1987. *Introduction of recombinant DNA-engineered organisms into the environment: Key issues*. Washington, D.C.: National Academy Press.

National Research Council (U.S.). 1983. *Acid deposition: Atmospheric processes in eastern North America: A scientific understanding*. Washington, D.C.: National Academy Press.

———. 1986. *Ecological knowledge and environmental problem-solving*. Washington, D.C.: National Academy Press.

Newmark, W. D. 1987. A land-bridge island perspective in mammalian extinctions in western North American parks. *Nature* 325:430–32.

Odum, E. P. 1971. *Fundamentals of ecology*, 3rd ed. Philadelphia: Saunders.

Odum, W. E. 1982. Environmental degradation and the tyranny of small decisions. *BioScience* 32:728–29.

Office of Technology Assessment (U.S.A.). 1987. *Wastes in the marine environment*. Washington, D.C.: O.T.A.

Paine, R. T. 1974. Intertidal community structure: Experimental studies on the relationship between a dominant competitor and its principal predator. *Oecologia* 15:93–120.

———. 1980. Food webs: Linkage, interaction strength and community infrastructure. *J. Anim. Ecol.* 49:667–85.

Patin, S. A. 1982. *Pollution and the biological resources of the oceans*. London: Butterworths.

Peters, R., ed. 1989. *The consequences of worldwide warming to global biodiversity*. New Haven: Yale Univ. Press.

Postel, S. 1984. Air pollution, acid rain and the future of forests. *Worldwatch Paper* 58:1–22, 44–49.

Quinn, J. F., C. van Riper, III, and H. Salwasser. 1988. Mammalian extinctions in the United States. Ms. subm. to *Oecologia*.

Raven, P. H. 1976. Ethics and attitudes. Pp. 155–79 in Simmons, J. B., R. I. Beyer, R. E. Brandham, G. L. Lucas, and V. T. H. Parry, eds., *Conservation of threatened plants*. New York: Plenum.

Ray, G. C. 1988. Ecological diversity in coastal zones and oceans. Pp. 36–50 in Wilson, 1988.

Regal, P. J. 1986. Models of genetically engineered organisms and their ecological impact. Pp. 111–29 in Mooney and Drake, 1986.

Schiff, A. L. 1962. *Fire and water—Scientific heresy in the Forest Service*. Cambridge, Mass.: Harvard Univ. Press.

Seal, U. S. 1988. Intensive technology in the care of ex situ populations of vanishing species. Pp. 289–95 in Wilson, 1988.

Shaffer, M. L. 1981. Minimum population sizes for species conservation. *BioScience* 31:131–34.

Shelford, V. E. 1913. *Animal communities in temperate America*. Chicago: Univ. of Chicago Press.

Simberloff, D. 1980. A succession of paradigms in ecology: Essentialism to materialism and probabilism. *Synthese* 43:3–39.

―――. 1987. The spotted owl fracas: Mixing academic, applied, and political ecology. *Ecology* 68:766–72.

―――. 1988. The contributions of population and community biology to conservation science. *Annu. Rev. Ecol. Syst.* 19:473–511.

Soulé, M. E. 1980. Thresholds for survival: Maintaining fitness and evolutionary potential. Pp. 111–24 in Soulé, M. E., and B. A. Wilcox, eds., *Conservation biology: An evolutionary-ecological perspective.* Sunderland, Mass.: Sinauer.

Soulé, M. E., ed. 1986. *Conservation biology: The science of scarcity and diversity.* Sunderland, Mass.: Sinauer.

―――. 1987. *Viable populations for conservation.* Cambridge: Cambridge Univ. Press.

Soulé, M. E., B. A. Wilcox, and C. Holtby. 1979. Benign neglect: A model of faunal collapse in the game reserves of East Africa. *Biol. Conserv.* 15:259–72.

Temple, S. A. 1981. Applied island biogeography and the conservation of endangered island birds in the Indian Ocean. *Biol. Conserv.* 20:147–61.

Terborgh, J. 1975. Faunal equilibria and the design of wildlife preserves. Pp. 369–80 in Golley, F., and E. Medina, eds., *Tropical ecological systems: Trends in terrestrial and aquatic research.* New York: Springer.

―――. 1986. Keystone plant resources in the tropical forest. Pp. 330–44 in Soulé, 1986.

Verner, J., M. L. Morrison, and C. J. Ralph. 1986. *Wildlife 2000.* Madison, Wis.: Univ. of Wisconsin Press.

Vitousek, P. M. 1986. Biological invasions and ecosystem properties: Can species make a difference? Pp. 163–76 in Mooney and Drake, 1986.

―――. 1988. Diversity and biological invasions of oceanic islands. Pp. 181–89 in Wilson, 1988.

Whittaker, R. H. 1956. Vegetation of the Great Smoky Mountains. *Ecol. Monogr.* 26:1–80.

―――. 1967. Gradient analysis of vegetation. *Biol. Rev.* 42:207–64.

Wilford, J. N. 1987. Intense scientific efforts fail to reverse Panda's decline. *New York Times,* March 17.

Wilson, E. O. 1988. *Biodiversity.* Washington, D.C.: National Academy Press.

Wilson, E. O., and E. O. Willis. 1975. Applied biogeography. Pp. 523–34 in Cody, M. L., and J. M. Diamond, eds., *Ecology and evolution of communities.* Cambridge, Mass.: Harvard Univ. Press.

Zedler, J. B. 1988. Restoring diversity in salt marshes. Can we do it? Pp. 317–25 in Wilson, 1988.

Zimmerman, B. L., and R. O. Bierregaard. 1986. Relevance of the equilibrium theory of island biogeography and species-area relations to conservation with a case from Amazonia. *J. Biogeogr.* 13:133–143.

8 Conservation Leadership in Academia

JAMES E. CROWFOOT
Dean, School of Natural Resources, The University of Michigan

SINCE THE END of the nineteenth century, U.S. colleges and universities have contributed directly to the cause of conservation through teaching and research. Many of these institutions began this work in response to natural resource degradation. Here in Michigan, where I have taught and done research, it was the cutting of the vast white pine forests that gave rise to the need for education in forestry and conservation. Now, well over a half century later, the cause of conservation faces a global crisis that is unprecedented in human history. What can academia offer to help respond to the ever-worsening natural resource and environmental problems?

I write from the vantage point of sixteen years' experience as a faculty member in a college of natural resources where, since 1983, I have served as dean. During this time, I have been directly associated with the development of new academic programs and research projects, and most recently with organizational redirection in response to the changing societal priorities of the 1980s. I have been involved in the education of a steady stream of bright and creative students who went on to work in natural resource and environmental management. My experience has also included work with citizens' groups that seek to bring new directions and energy to the cause of conservation in the United States.

There are other important perspectives that I do not possess: the perspectives of environmental activists, of academic leaders outside of the environmental field, and of faculty who come from different backgrounds than my own social science and interdisciplinary experience. Discussion of this chapter, along with the opportunities for formulation of other understandings, is thus needed to ensure that the conservation movement benefits from a broader set of perspectives on what academia has to offer to this movement.

While I am aware of the gap between current academic programs and the severity of the environmental problems we face, I am hopeful that academic institutions will respond positively to society's needs for new expertise and leadership. Such a response will require an effective partnership with organizations and leaders from outside academia who have direct involvement with environmental and natural resource management, societal planning, and policy-making. For such a partnership to happen, it is essential that academics describe from their perspective:

1. What academia has to contribute to the conservation movement.
2. Conditions affecting academia's contribution to the conservation movement.
3. Emerging directions and potential contributions of higher education to the conservation movement.
4. Challenges and problems to be addressed as academia seeks to contribute to the future of the conservation movement.

The time is right for academia to focus on the changes it can make to help address the emerging crisis. On December 13, 1988, the national academies of sciences of the United States and the Soviet Union announced the formation of a Joint Committee on Global Ecology. This indicates the seriousness with which the scientific community views global environmental problems. The statement issued with this announcement of joint action said: "The consequences of the rapid growth of our population coupled with global economic development now pose a significant threat to our continued existence" (*New York Times,* 12/14/88, p. 7).

Contributions from Academia

The central mission of academic organizations is to teach and educate, research and discover. Quite often they are requested to provide other services. For example, they might consult with property owners who want help in cleaning up pollution or train groups of managers in the techniques and standards needed to clean up a hazardous waste spill. These are legitimate and important needs, but they are outside the central mission of colleges and universities.

On occasion, academic organizations will undertake such tasks, sometimes for reasons that honor their central mission—for example, to develop new knowledge in the context of a limited project that is not available to researchers unless it is operated by the academic unit. Alternatively, such activities may be a necessary element of the curriculum because they provide learner roles for students that are unavailable in any other way. In other cases, specific projects or subunits are created in response to governmental mandates and funding. The cooperative extension units of land-grant universities are examples. In each of these situations, the central mission of colleges and universities is honored and the activities are ancillary to the main activities of academia.

In addressing what academia can contribute to leadership in the conservation movement, the central mission of colleges and universities needs to be understood and honored. Failure to do so will result in the conservation movement getting less than it deserves from academic organizations, and perhaps having ongoing disputes with them. The conservation movement will gain greater assistance from academia if it focuses on the research and instructional capabilities of colleges and universities.

The ever-growing crisis in the natural environment gives rise to important needs that are within the central mission of academic organizations. One of these needs is for new knowledge. Continued research is needed in the following areas:

1. Basic biophysical and sociobehavioral sciences, to advance scientific understanding of the systems, processes, and organisms that constitute the biosphere.
2. Applied environmental and natural resource science, to understand processes of change and interventions to alter such processes.
3. Humanities-centered works of philosophy, ethics, arts, literature, and religion, to envision and articulate new cultural meanings and practices relating humans and the natural environment.
4. Policy and management strategies and practices, to change the relationships between natural environments and human social systems.

Academia should be doing more original research and scholarship in each of these areas while synthesizing existing research on specific environmental problems. The conservation movement could assist by advocating such research and by expressing its views of priority needs for new knowledge and syntheses in each of these four areas. Academia should be doing a better job of disseminating the results of its scholarship on the environment. At the same time, the conservation movement could improve its work on environmental problems by recognizing the need for research-based information to guide the implementation of practices that will lessen environmental problems. In the heat of crisis and with the energy and commitment of a movement, it is all too easy to act in ways that are well intentioned but ill informed, and that do not result in the intended effects.

A second major need of the conservation movement is for more and better-educated people in each of the following three areas:

1. Doctorate-level researchers and teachers who are specialized in natural resources and the environment (for example, ecologists, natural resource and environmental economists, and environmental psychologists).
2. Professional practitioners who are specialized in the various fields of environmental and natural resource science, policy,

planning, and management (for example, environmental planners, forest and water managers, landscape architects, and environmental policy analysts).

3. College-educated citizens who have a basic understanding of environmental and natural resource problems and a commitment to solving them.

Colleges and universities need to improve their degree programs and curricula for students in each of these areas. In general, the need is for greatly expanding the number of students who are being taught what the realities of the environmental challenge are and how to effect changes that result in sustainable use of the world's resources.

But the challenge is more than just the numbers of students being educated. Formal education must also contribute to the commitment to bring about change through effective problem solving. Accomplishing these outcomes requires innovation in curricula and teaching. The conservation movement can play a vital role in advocating the need for more and better educational programs focused on the environment. It also can be a valued partner in shaping changes in programs and curricula and in helping to recruit the most talented and committed people into these programs.

The conservation movement needs continuing education programs. Many conservation activists do not have the knowledge to fulfill their goals and responsibilities. Our understanding of environmental problems continues to change rapidly; conservationists thus need to update their knowledge of critical problems such as global warming, deforestation, hazardous waste management, and population growth. As the environmental crisis deepens, continuing education will be a vital component of efforts to ameliorate impacts and address underlying causes.

Colleges and universities have long recognized the need for lifelong education, since many individuals will have more than one career. This recognition has been more at the level of rhetoric than in programs to address this need. There have been few such programs focusing on the environment and natural resources. The conservation movement needs to be an active partner in diagnosing needs for continuing education and helping to shape the programs and courses that will respond to these needs.

Influences on Academia's Response to the Movement's Needs

To gain from academia more and better contributions to reducing environmental problems requires an understanding of existing natural resource programs and a deeper appreciation of the changes in higher education that are influencing them. To many activists, the goals, priorities, and politics of academic organizations are frustrating bureaucratic concerns that they would prefer to ignore. For better or worse, organizational constraints and opportunities in higher education must be mastered in order to gain a greater academic contribution to the conservation movement.

THE PRESENT SITUATION

Three characteristics of natural resource and environmental programs most greatly affect their ability to provide high-quality research and education.

First, environmental topics have not been a concern of the basic academic disciplines (such as biology, chemistry, mathematics, political science, and psychology) that constitute the traditional core of colleges and universities. In most disciplines, environmental problems have long been ignored. What is more, environmental matters have not been identified with a single discipline. One result is that academic units focused on the environment and natural resources have their organizational niche outside the colleges of literature, science, and the arts. Environmental programs have been the domain of professional schools, research institutes, cross-disciplinary concentrations, and interdisciplinary programs. Given that such units are usually of a much lower priority than disciplinary departments, natural resource programs are usually small and inadequately funded. Their capacity to do research and educate students is limited, and their peripheral status makes them more vulnerable to shifts in the priorities of colleges and universities.

Not every university or college has a program specifically focused on natural resources. Where such programs exist, they occupy very different positions in the structures of their respective institutions. To many academic administrators, these units at best are difficult to understand and at worst are expendable.

Second, society's cyclical interest in these programs diminishes their offerings. Historically in the United States, there have been very marked shifts in interest in environmental problems; this has affected higher education along with many other sectors. Rapid shifts in student enrollment have accompanied employment opportunities and the status of careers in natural resource fields. Since World War II and the development of the full-blown research university, major swings in levels of government research funding have also affected academic natural resource programs. The result has been a series of rollercoaster rides for the programs.

The early and middle 1970s were boom times for environmental and natural resource units, but the late 1970s and 1980s brought a bust. As the downturn occurred, many academic natural resource programs suffered budget and personnel reductions. In my own college, the university in 1982 reduced the budget of the School of Natural Resources by more than 20 percent in response to reductions in governmental funding. One result was a decrease in research expenditures; enrollments also plummeted from a high of 925 in the late 1970s to a low of 360 in 1983. While the exact magnitude of these decreases and their timing differed among colleges and universities, the overall pattern of substantially fewer students and reduced budgets was similar. Such instabilities harm the curriculum and research programs and lead to employment uncertainties for faculty and staff. They also diminish the units' status on campus and their ability to sustain interunit programs and other important collaborative relationships.

The third characteristic that greatly affects academic natural re-source programs is their cost coupled with the typical salaries re-ceived by graduates who specialize in these fields. The programs tend to be expensive because their curricula and research require state-of-the-art biophysical science laboratories and field research capabilities. Moreover, many of these units are increasingly interdisciplinary and thus require intense commitments of faculty time and resources. Often they include landscape design and regional planning studios with the attendant computer equipment and simulation and model-building capabilities. The advent of remote sensing and geographic information systems as important new tools for resource manage-ment has required new and expensive equipment and facilities. All of these represent costs that go well beyond the familiar lecture halls and discussion rooms which are the sole requirements of many less ex-pensive academic areas. These needs drive up tuition and complicate negotiations for the scarce dollars allocated among competing units.

The graduates of environmental and natural resource programs generally earn less than physicians, business executives, and lawyers; thus, they cannot take on the levels of debt that graduates in other areas can. The results are obvious: The necessarily higher levels of student financial aid exacerbate the problem of rising costs in higher education. Students become less able to enroll, and the units face in-creasing difficulty in recruiting.

At the same time, natural resource and environmental units have not been able to build up the endowments or patterns of annual giv-ing found in schools of business, law, medicine, and engineering that would provide the needed levels of financial aid. This is due to the modest giving capabilities of most alumni of these programs coupled with the low level of societal philanthropy that has been devoted to environmental concerns, particularly as those concerns are expressed through academic programs. Historically, these units have not had fund-raising programs and have placed a low priority on generating their own financial resources.

One answer is to expect colleges and universities to allocate money to meet this need or, as critics would put it, to subsidize some units from the monies that could be going to medicine, engineering, law, and business administration.

CHANGES IN HIGHER EDUCATION

Changes occurring in higher education will impact environmental and natural resource units and their ability to be of assistance to the conservation movement. These include the rising costs of higher education, increasing pressure on colleges and universities to assist in economic development and national defense, increasing emphasis on centers of excellence, reduced numbers of high school graduates, and pressures to achieve greater diversity within the student group and the faculty.

The costs of colleges and universities are increasing much more rapidly than the standard of living. At the same time, governmental support of higher education is declining. Most units are charging higher tuition. More and more students must decide where they will attend college based on their ability to pay; the level of student indebtedness is rapidly increasing. These changes will make it more difficult to attract the most talented and committed young people into natural resource and environmental careers. Cost-conscious colleges and universities will have to make very difficult decisions on priorities; the centrality, quality, and cost of particular programs will influence these decisions.

Historically, the centrality of specific programs has been tied to academic disciplinary traditions and the need to respond to societal needs, particularly for economic development and national security. To date, environmental and natural resource programs do not fit within disciplinary traditions, nor have they been considered necessary components of efforts to advance economic development and national security. In the scramble for the ever-scarce financial resources of their parent organizations, natural resource and environmental programs are thus greatly disadvantaged. A hopeful sign is found in new and more innovative research in which the natural environment is viewed as central to development and security.

Competitive pressures and declining resources are forcing universities to support their key areas of excellence and strength at the expense of lower-priority programs. Often, the environmental and natural resource units, because of their historically small size and lack of centrality, are not given the highest priority.

In the face of diminishing funding for higher education, the size of student enrollments is important. Tuition revenues will be an ever more important contributor to academic budgets. The declining numbers of high school graduates will continue to increase competition for enrollees among various environmental and natural resource programs, and between these programs and other academic areas seeking to attract students.

With changing U.S. and global demographics, the racial makeup of colleges and universities is also changing. People of color will constitute an increasing proportion of the U.S. and global populations; they are not presently represented in higher education at the levels of their numbers in society. Changes are called for in the makeup of student bodies, faculties, and administrations. Beyond changes in numbers, there are pressing needs for changes in organizational culture and curricula to reduce racism and include the perspectives, methods, and concerns of nonwhite citizens. These changes will strongly affect environmental and natural resources programs, which continue to be overwhelmingly white.

There is also intense pressure to increase the number of women in university faculties and administrations. This trend, too, requires alteration of the organizational culture and curricula. Sexism is a major societal and global issue; the conflict surrounding it shows every indication of intensifying. There are growing numbers of female students in environmental and natural resource programs, but as yet few women in the faculty. This pattern will necessitate change and bring conflict.

Emerging Directions and Their Contributions

The changes that are now occurring in natural resource and environmental units fall into four categories: curricula, program emphases, collaborative relationships, and strategies for acquiring resources. The following descriptions are based on my own experience and therefore are not exhaustive.

CURRICULUM CHANGES

Most environmental and natural resource programs now seek to strengthen students' scientific training. The complexity of environmental programs demands that students and professionals have a stronger scientific foundation. More mathematics and more physical, natural, and social sciences are now prerequisites or corequirements for courses in natural resources. The needed changes are blunted by the low level of high school students' interest in science and the problems of science and mathematics instruction at the high school level.

Budget reductions and declining enrollments have led to reductions in the total numbers of natural resource and environmental courses. In 1988 and 1989, however, there were renewed signs of growing student interest in environmental offerings. The interest will have to swell for several years before it results in major additions to curricula.

Some curricula increasingly recognize the interdisciplinary nature of environmental and natural resource problems. Problems such as hazardous and solid waste management, atmospheric deposition, ecosystem management, and forest planning cannot be adequately understood without the expertise of several disciplines, and certainly not reduced without interdisciplinary problem solving.

While environmental studies programs from their beginnings were interdisciplinary, most natural resource and environmental science programs were not. Environmental studies programs arose in the 1970s from the interests of individual faculty members and students from the biological, physical, and social sciences, along with the humanities, coming together to focus on environmental problems. Natural resource programs were started in the early 1900s by faculty in forestry, fisheries, and wildlife. Environmental science programs were started in the 1960s and 1970s and focused on the needs of the biophysical sciences and technology development in response to environmental problems. Natural resource and environmental science programs increasingly include electives and requirements for inter-disciplinary courses, seminars, and projects. This trend of providing for substantive diversity continues to grow despite recent counter-pressures toward fewer course offerings and added requirements related to field of specialization.

While professional specialization in such areas as forestry, wildlife, landscape architecture, and outdoor recreation historically occurred at the undergraduate level, it is now offered at the master's level. The progress of this trend varies among different professional areas; for example, it is just beginning in forestry but is widespread in land-scape architecture. This important change grows out of both the recognition of the complexity of environmental problems and the desirability of having sound undergraduate preparation prior to pro-fessional specialization. While the trend will result in better-educated professionals, it also requires that students incur greater costs for their education, since more will have to attend graduate school.

There is also more attention being paid to experiential education, including field studies and internships. Unlike their predominantly rural counterparts from earlier decades, most students entering nat-ural resource programs today come from urban and suburban back-grounds. They need opportunities to live and study in the field for concentrated periods of time. Biological field stations and natural re-source camps are expensive for colleges and universities to develop and maintain. Some universities have eliminated them. Many pro-grams and curricula are now sharing facilities. When field programs occur in the summer, as is generally the case, students have to forgo summer employment, making these experiences particularly costly for them.

As curricula increasingly include more basic science and laboratory-based instruction, there remains an unmet need for stu-dents to have practical work experiences focused on reducing envi-ronmental problems. Such opportunities are needed in both the pri-vate and public sectors and in settings that range from local to federal to international. Curricula will increasingly provide for these. Here again, many of these experiences will take place in the summer months. A challenge will be for them to include adequate compensation for students. In addition to university programs, nonprofit organizations such as the Student Conservation Association and the Center for Environment and Internship Programs (CEIP, Inc.) are expanding to place students in internships.

Graduate-level curricula will increasingly require courses in both disciplinary departments and the professional environmental programs. Developing and maintaining curricula that cross these often impermeable boundaries is difficult but absolutely necessary to provide students with the strongest possible education.

Leaders from the conservation movement could participate in curriculum development and bring to it their priorities and experiences. This will occur most easily when faculty members also have experience in and commitment to the environmental movement. Where faculty do not have the background or commitment, other means—such as external advisory committees and national studies of needed environmental leadership—must be created to gain the input of professional practitioners, scientists, and volunteer leaders of the movement. The conservation movement needs to take the initiative to create a dialogue on curriculum with academic leaders.

PROGRAM CHANGES

Other important changes in natural resource programs are also occurring. One new direction is to provide more education on international environmental and natural resource problems, including a new focus on less-developed countries and on global problems such as climate change and ozone depletion, which will affect all parts of the world. Both United States and non–United States students are seeking such emphases. These program changes require attention to different ecosystems from those found in the United States. Cross-cultural studies are also vital components. More attention must be given to socioeconomic diversity than is typical of most domestically focused programs. Language training and area studies become very important in new programs focusing on non-U.S. environmental problems. These changes will require faculty with different training, new courses and curricula, and new collaborative relationships inside and outside the university. New arrangements for financial aid will also be necessary to assist foreign students.

Some new programs derive directly from technological changes affecting environmental and natural resource management. Many are based on developments in computer science and computer applications. The growing use of geographic information systems, for example, is beginning to stimulate complementary changes in academic programs. The growth of artificial intelligence technologies will also affect the education of specialists in natural resources.

Other new programs will arise as well due to emerging domestic environmental concerns. Human health and the environment, the restoration of damaged ecosystems, biophysical diversity, new approaches to solid waste management, and indoor environmental pollution are examples of new programs or emphases that will require interdisciplinary collaboration as well as effective relationships with professional practitioners and policymakers.

New Collaborative Relationships

The expanding scope and urgency of environmental problems demands the involvement of more organizations and individuals. Occurring in the context of fiscal austerity, the growing crisis nonetheless calls for expanded capabilities and new levels of efficiency in addressing these problems. Joining the forces of previously separated and unrelated organizations and programs will become the norm rather than the exception. Both the amount and the quality of inter-organizational collaboration will change. The conservation movement will help shape and participate in the resulting arrangements.

One type of collaboration that promises to expand rapidly in the near future is the interunit instructional program. In some instances, units are established with the mission of fostering interdisciplinary collaboration in environmental problems. The University of Wisconsin's Institute for Environmental Studies is a model for this way of achieving collaboration. It is a freestanding unit with the mission and capacity to enlist interested faculty from throughout the arts and sciences as well as the departments of the agricultural college. In other instances of collaboration, previously separate programs join forces due to a recognition of real-world interactions that are poorly understood. One example is the University of Michigan's new Population and Environment Dynamics Program, which links the School of Public Health's population work with the School of Natural Resources' environmental work. Another example of this type of cooperation is the new Wetlands Center at Duke University, located in the School of Forestry and Environmental Studies, but with the interdisciplinary support of Duke's Institute for Policy Sciences and Public Affairs and its schools of law, business, and engineering. In other instances, collaborations grow out of the application of new technologies to environmental problems. For instance, the use of geographic information systems is resulting in new collaborative relationships among urban planning, population studies, archaeology, anthropology, geology, engineering, natural resources, the research library, field biology, and other specialties.

New research institutes and instructional units will emerge as a result of increased interdisciplinary collaboration to work on environmental problems. It is hoped that more effective and efficient administrative arrangements will accompany the emerging pattern of collaboration and contribute to, rather than impede, solutions to these problems in the world. The conservation movement should be alert to opportunities for influencing the new developments in higher education. Opportunities include new multiparty research initiatives with environmental nonprofits as one of the parties, joint sponsorship of seminars and conferences addressing critical environmental problems, joint appointments of research scientists, and new adjunct faculty roles for professionals from environmental nonprofit organizations.

Interuniversity research projects, which assemble new scientific teams and the research-support facilities of several institutions, are emerging now in several states. Funders who see a gap between research needs and available funds view interuniversity projects as more effective means to use limited money. Decision makers in both the public and private sectors see them as valuable ways to surmount competition while aggregating expertise and other resources that do not exist within a single college or university.

A recent example of interuniversity research is the National Center for Geographic Information and Analysis—a joint venture of the State University of New York at Buffalo, the University of California at Santa Barbara, and the University of Maine at Orono. A smaller example growing out of three different forestry programs is occurring in Michigan, where a scientific team composed of faculty and research scientists from the University of Michigan, Michigan State University, and Michigan Technological University is studying the impacts of atmospheric pollution on terrestrial ecosystems along a pollution gradient extending from northwestern Ohio to northwestern Michigan. Funding is coming from federal, state, and private sources.

Given the small sizes and budgets of most natural resource units on any single campus, there is significant potential for interuniversity collaboration. New communications technology contributes to the potential for active day-to-day communication by students and faculty across several campuses. Nevertheless, collaboration faces barriers in faculty membership, degree requirements, tuition levels, and traditions of competition and autonomy.

New programs can be expected that involve academic organizations, government, nonprofits, and private-sector groups. These will grow from a desire to combine the strengths of several organizations. For example, the International Seminar on Forest Planning and Administration is a joint effort of the U.S.D.A. Forest Service and the School of Natural Resources of the University of Michigan. Its traveling seminar for forestry leaders from third-world countries could not be operated by either one of these organizations alone.

There is a history of cooperative units involving academia, government, and the private sector that focus on specific natural resource problems such as spruce budworm infestation, wildlife management, and northern hardwoods management. More such cooperative ventures can be expected in the future, and some of these will involve the new regional structures of joint resource planning and management, such as a current one involving the Great Lakes states and provinces working to protect the water quality of the Great Lakes or one involving Minnesota, Michigan, and Wisconsin in the management of the northern forests.

It is hoped that some of these expanded and new collaborative relationships will involve academic organizations in the United States and their counterparts in developing countries. The potential for such relationships lies in promoting mutual interdependence that expands the capabilities of each involved unit and improves the sharing of scarce expertise, equipment, and other resources. While a few such collaborative relationships now exist, they are the exception rather than the rule. The more typical pattern is one of short-term collaborative projects involving students from developing countries attending U.S. colleges and universities.

New Resource Strategies

Finding the needed funding, expertise, space, and equipment for the rapid expansion of environmental and natural resource research and instructional programs is going to be a major challenge. The new resource strategies have two objectives: (1) attracting more dollars to research and education focused on environmental problems and (2) utilizing available dollars more effectively in environmental education and research.

Academic units focused on these critical societal and global problems must increase monies coming from present funders and gain the help of new ones. The theme is self-sufficiency. To be effective in pursuit of these increased levels of support will require greater competitiveness based on the societal importance of the education and research being done, the numbers and the quality of students enrolled, and the quality of the research. At the same time, these units need to enlist new donors. This will require making the case for the importance of academic work on environmental and natural resource problems, and the value of the education and research being per-formed.

As academic units pursue these strategies, they will cooperate and compete with other organizations in the conservation movement. The competition will occur as academic organizations seek contri-butions from some of the same donors who have traditionally sup-ported environmental nonprofits. Such competition could have pos-itive effects if the fund-raising attracts substantial numbers of larger gifts from old donors and increases the number of new donors to environmental causes. Efforts are badly needed to reduce the lag time between discovering and applying new knowledge in the policy-making and management arenas and the gap between theory and practice in the education of natural resource professionals. This is the overriding reason for academics and conservation advocates to be collaborating.

If the emphasis is on "expanding the pie" of private dollars, coop-erative strategies and fund-raising efforts could be pursued by aca-demic units in concert with environmental and other public interest organizations. Environmental organizations want to increase the numbers of students receiving an environmental education and help improve the quality of the education they receive. Similarly, these organizations recognize the need for new research. Their own efforts to address problems require better information and expertise. Aca-demic organizations should be able to recognize the importance of environmental advocacy groups as well as governmental and private sector organizations that work to reduce environmental problems. These organizations offer the means by which public attention and support are drawn to efforts to improve environmental quality and achieve sustainable patterns of natural resource use. Academic orga-nizations committed to the environment benefit from such public support as well as from effective ongoing efforts to improve the en-vironment. Academics have higher respect for advocacy organiza-tions that make an effort to identify and use relevant scientific find-ings and in so doing base their actions and appeals on facts as well as emotions.

Strategies for improving resource acquisition for the academic organizations allied with the conservation movement must also focus on attracting the best students and faculty. State-of-the-art enrollment management strategies will be used increasingly. Competitive faculty salaries are essential, but of equal relevance is the excitement and attractiveness of the instructional and research programs seeking new personnel.

Finding new resources will depend heavily on enhancing program effectiveness and organizational efficiency. Universities must evolve to understand that efficiency fosters the sustainable use of environmental resources—one of the key values of academic units focused on the environment. As the environmental crisis deepens and resource reallocations occur, many sectors of society will be forced to pursue greater efficiency and effectiveness. Support for work in natural resources will be greater if the organizations can demonstrate their own success in improving the efficiency and effectiveness of their own programs.

Academic natural resource and environmental programs will need to master strategies for becoming high-productivity organizations. As they do so, it is essential that they incorporate values stressing balance, health, and sustainability. It is all too easy for these organizations to be crisis-driven, narrow in purpose, and stressful. These organizations face a major challenge in seeking to be highly productive while at the same time enhancing the well-being of their members and contributing to the sustainable use of the natural environment. If academic organizations are able to do this, they could serve as models to organizations in the conservation movement.

Universities must also avoid duplication of programs; involve volunteers; initiate new joint ventures with other academic and nonacademic organizations; and use state-of-the-art tools for organizational communication, fiscal management, and decision making. Faced with overextended budgets and buoyed with new commitments to be effective partners in the struggle to solve environmental problems, academic organizations must reverse their tendencies toward tradition and inertia. The challenges to these organizations will increase as environmental problems continue to expand in scope and urgency.

Challenges and Problems

Academia could benefit from the ideas and recommendations of the conservation movement as it seeks to resolve several difficult and important challenges. I have grouped these challenges into three categories:

1. The assumptions, focus, and boundaries of instruction and research on the environment and natural resources.
2. The goals, directions, and forms of specific academic programs of research and instruction.
3. The values of higher-education organizations in relation to the natural environment and the society on which they depend.

ASSUMPTIONS, FOCUS, AND BOUNDARIES

As with any other area of intellectual inquiry, natural resource studies have been shaped by forces from both within and outside of academia. Rapid changes continue to occur.

Throughout the nineteenth and early twentieth centuries (the life span of most of U.S. higher education), the natural environment was taken as a given that did not require special attention. In some regions of the country, however, acute environmental problems spawned new departments or university programs with a focus on natural resources, but in the main, higher education ignored the natural environment. Today this is no longer so true; in the future, virtually all parts of colleges and universities will be concerned with the environment and natural resources. The foundation of life on our planet is in peril.

As the crisis progresses, fundamental cultural and intellectual premises will be redefined, including the definitions of environment and natural resources. In the future these topics will not be as separated and as distinguishable as they have been up to now. Everyone seeking to address these matters in higher education and elsewhere will be challenged to understand what is an environmental issue. As this occurs, strictly biophysical phenomena will be included, but matters of human groups and individual behavior as well as human cultural phenomena will come to be equally understood as environmental matters. It is clear now that environmental problems require the theories, methods, and findings of multiple disciplines. The pressure for interdisciplinary environmental problem solving in both curricula and research programs will continue to increase. Teachers and researchers for the most part have not been educated to work in this way. Current college and university reward systems often do not recognize and rarely encourage interdisciplinary work.

New definitions of environmental problems and problem solving will bring major changes to academic programs and organizations. Some changes will be in the content and structure of programs. Others will flow from the crisis character of the forces stimulating change and will raise new questions about the relationships among problems. Anticipating and coping with these changes present new challenges to colleges and universities, and certainly for those administrators, faculty, and students who focus on the environment. Ultimately, universities will be asked to help answer the profound question of the twenty-first century: What is the meaning of sustainability and how can it be accomplished?

Historically, university programs in natural resources have been shaped by commodity groups interested in making a profit from the environment. The growing concern with environmental impacts and the destruction of ecosystems and species are bringing unprecedented attention to preservation and nonconsumptive uses of the environment and its resources. Mission statements and organizational cultures must be changed in response to this important societal reinterpretation of the environmental imperative. Making such changes rapidly in academic organizations is very difficult and will require high levels of commitment to the processes of deliberate organizational change.

Are environmental and natural resource problems primarily local, regional, national, or global in character? Until quite recently, most academic programs focused on regional problems and to a lesser extent national problems. Some research and instruction emphasized local and international environmental issues, but these have been of secondary importance. Today there is a rapidly shifting understanding of the answer to this question, and with this change has come the recognition of the importance of global environmental problems.

Responding to this change will require universities to address cross-cultural communication and collaboration as essential elements of work on the natural environment. Area studies and languages become essential inputs to natural resource programs that seek to respond to global environmental problems. Ethnocentrism stands as a major obstacle to programs with an international focus.

Historically, the overwhelming majority of faculty and students in these programs were white and male. Increasing numbers of women students and faculty are entering natural resource programs, but the color barrier remains. Racism is beginning to be perceived as a problem in natural resource programs. But there is an immense gap between recognition and change that will alter the student and faculty composition of these programs, their curricula and course content, as well as the organizational culture that affects day-to-day interactions. With the rapidly increasing proportion of blacks, Hispanics, Native Americans, and Asian Americans in the United States, and given the fact that people of color are the majority in the world, academia will feel relentless pressure to respond. Natural resource and environmental programs have perhaps the longest way to go.

Worldwide, women are generally more concerned with environmental problems than men. Women probably will play an increasingly important role in solving these problems. Sexism is still alive and well in academic organizations, including natural resource and environmental units. Because of the increased numbers of female students, this problem will continue to increase in importance.

New environmental and natural resource problem solving will have to accommodate such diversity and use it as a positive resource for creativity, sophisticated analysis, collaborative decision making, and systematic processes of change. Academic units will be called upon to pioneer new solutions that employ the insights of multiple cultures and races, women and men, and different intellectual fields and traditions.

To date, academic work on environmental problems has stressed scientific analysis. This mode of analysis brings with it powerful tools and essential results, but with the advent of deep ecology, other modes of analysis are needed to cultivate an appreciation and love of the environment as well as an orientation and intuition that are a part of nature itself. The humanities have not been a direct participant in natural resource programs. Nonscientific methods that embrace subjective experiences of the environment and use traditions such as art, music, and mysticism have not found a home in very many academic settings. Academic programs need to embrace the full array of methods for understanding and appreciating nature and for altering human relationships to the natural environment. Relying exclusively on scientific methods is no longer viable. These are valuable and powerful, but bring with them the weaknesses of detachment and control and do not provide adequate means for a holistic understanding of the biosphere.

Traditionally, universities have sought to separate scholarship from action, but in the face of the growing environmental crisis, this pattern of academic life will be increasingly challenged. Should environmental and natural resource programs take the lead in resource conservation and recycling on campus? Do these programs bear any special responsibilities of leadership in efforts to reduce environmental problems? If these programs deliberately forge a new relationship between theory/research and decision making/practice, what should this relationship be? What protections of good scholarship need to be built in? What provisions need to be made to ensure that the conditions of the policy-making and management arenas are valued parts of academic programs?

Any of these challenges would be sufficient for environmental academic programs to grapple with in the next twenty years. But the reality is that all these and more are what we face because of the global crisis that is upon us. Effective responses to these challenges will require exceptional creativity and commitment to experiment and change. Leadership will be a key requirement for achieving these changes. What should this leadership be like, and where should it come from?

GOALS, DIRECTIONS, AND FORMS

The conservation movement needs to approach higher education through leader-to-leader contact, with the expectation of fostering strategic approaches to operating natural resource and environmental units. The instruction and research of these units will help alleviate environmental problems, inform a new vision of human and environment interactions, and achieve a deeper understanding of the natural environment and all the interactions that affect it. Higher education prepares the next generation of societal leaders and shapes the knowledge base from which leaders and members of society operate. For the conservation movement not to exercise influence on higher education and work actively with colleges and universities on goals, structures, and programs would be extremely shortsighted.

Leaders in higher education need to identify the unique opportunities for improving instruction and research. Understanding institutional history, current commitments, and emerging directions is essential. No two colleges and universities are alike; what is done in the future with regard to environmental programs will be specific to each institution.

An era of unparalleled growth in higher education in the United States lasted from World War II until the 1970s, but now it is over. The strategic planning and management of environmental programs must occur as a part of internal reallocation and planned processes of change within colleges and universities. Advocates of these programs must learn to articulate their importance and communicate a vision and mission for academic work in environmental problems. Inevitably there will be conflict and resistance to change from interests that would further detach the university from involvement in societal problems and those that consider the environment to be merely one among many topics. Work in this milieu will be difficult but necessary for environmental and natural resource programs to gain the financial and intellectual resources they need. New collaborations with external partners in the public, private, and nonprofit sectors will be required to gain additional resources and provide for new combinations of theory and practice and new settings for applied research.

Each college and university needs to determine what it can do well in contributing to the reduction of environmental problems and helping to create a new vision of sustainable human interaction with the environment. To do this will require knowledge of peer academic programs and their plans for the future. Greater collaboration will be necessary to achieve this level of coordination and create opportunities to share resources. Currently, there are few mechanisms in place to foster planning and institutional cooperation among different natural resource and environmental programs.

Colleges and universities face the challenge of determining how they will use their resources to increase environmental literacy and educate new specialists. Every area of intellectual and professional life will be deeply affected by efforts to ameliorate environmental problems. Thus the opportunities for new academic initiatives are endless. Each institution will need to choose carefully what it does in order to make the best use of its financial and human resources to address these critical issues.

As this occurs, new collaborations between business and natural resource programs are possible. These will go beyond the past collaborations that trained a very small number of students working for both a master's in business administration and an M.S. in natural resources. New programs will seek to alter the fundamental premises of both professional areas. Such an altered perspective could be applied to myriad professions, including law, social work, library science, medicine, and others. Collaborations here also should involve the basic disciplines as well.

Implementing such ambitious plans will require new organizational structures and processes, facilitate joint activities, and provide flexibility to allow for expansion. There are no formulas or easy answers as to how this can be done or what goals and arrangements should be created. Creating such organizational arrangements will require creativity, courage, and leadership. One example of this needed leadership has come from Tufts University, where a dean for the environment has been given the responsibility to assist every unit in the university in paying attention to the natural environment and achieving changes that will ensure the environmental literacy of every student graduating from Tufts. The conservation movement can be a catalyst and a partner with faculty, students, and administrators who are committed to working on the environment.

VALUES IN RELATION TO THE NATURAL ENVIRONMENT AND SOCIETY

One traditional view of colleges and universities is that they are to remain "ivory towers"—places for thinking and scholarship, detached from the pressures and demands of society. Another view values these organizations for their "neutrality" in relation to controversial issues and "value-freeness" in relation to inquiry. It is now widely acknowledged, however, that colleges and universities cannot exist somehow apart from society and controversy. Indeed, they are embedded in society, and they are highly interdependent with other powerful organizations. Colleges and universities are not neutral, even when they decide to take no official position on controversial social and political issues. Scholars and their methods are never value free—despite rhetoric and claims to the contrary.

The challenge in the face of the deepening environmental crisis is for institutions of higher learning to establish explicit policies that acknowledge the crisis and the actions needed to alleviate it while establishing patterns of global sustainability. Failure to do so is tantamount to supporting the status quo and actively contributing to the fundamental crisis. If colleges and universities pursue this unfortunate course, they will become inhospitable places for environmental and natural resource educators and researchers, and will fail to provide leadership in the face of the threat to the biosphere.

To the extent that colleges and universities continue to promote the myth of value-free scholarship, they will inhibit the evolution of multiple methods of inquiry and synthesis, and fail to provide active debate on the relationship of various scholarly methods to the environmental crisis and what is needed to alleviate it. It is practically and morally suspect to continue the uncritical production of knowledge, methods, attitudes, and values that directly destroy the environment; ignore needed environmental protections; and fail to provide for sustainable, restorative use of natural resources. The community of scholars is challenged as never before to examine its biases and limitations of perspective in the face of exponential population growth, unsustainable economic growth, damaged and destroyed ecosystems, and technological impacts that threaten life. The prevailing goals, structures, and methods of higher education overwhelmingly support "business as usual," while our knowledge of the deepening environmental crisis calls for value and policy changes, new methods, new information and syntheses.

The challenge is to achieve major institutional changes that result in the redirection of resources in higher education toward efforts to reduce environmental problems and achieve a new and sustainable relationship between human and natural systems. Even this statement seems grandiose and impossibly difficult. But conservationists know that nothing less will do if we are to help achieve survival under new global conditions and if our children are to attain sustainable lifestyles in a global community.

9 Developing the Compleat Volunteer

JACK LORENZ
Executive Director, Izaak Walton League of America

"BEING A VOLUNTEER is one of the hardest jobs in the world. *Coordinating* volunteers is *the* hardest job in the world."

These words from Patricia Honeycutt, director of the Izaak Walton League of America's Public Lands Restoration Task Force in Portland, Oregon, summarize what many of us feel during a major environmental campaign that is dependent on the often incredible power of thousands of grass-roots conservationists.

The continual nurturing of volunteers, the constant balancing act between their needs and your needs, is a difficult factor in any organization. For those in the conservation movement, the effective use of volunteers and the day-to-day role these people play in environmental organizations are a topic of much debate. As an active participant in that debate for more than twenty years, I want to identify a few factors we all must consider.

First, the number of people seeking ways to *individually* help expand the earth's natural resources is skyrocketing. This rapid expansion of "the new green" has exposed serious weaknesses in how the movement utilizes the abilities and enthusiasm of volunteers, not only to supplement staff but to achieve long-term and short-term goals in environmental policy-making.

Are we, for instance, effectively matching volunteers' skills and needs with our wants? Are we providing adequate training for various tasks? Challenging volunteers as individuals? Giving them the freedom and responsibility to solve problems, offer ideas, and reap the rewards of personal—not just organizational—successes?

Are we further instilling a conservation ethic by educating volunteers as conservation leaders and in what they, as community role models, can do to solve environmental problems? Do we frequently honor and reward what one volunteer coordinator called "the hardest-working underpaid people we know"? Do we thank them publicly in our publications, at events, conventions, staff meetings, and any other times? No one I spoke with as I prepared this essay gave an absolute yes to any of these questions.

"There's a lot we do, and a lot more we ought to do," says Susan Carlson, program coordinator for regional and chapter activities at the National Audubon Society. "We should be motivating people to understand that there are huge obligations for us all, and that each one of us can make a difference."

"Motivating people," however, means not only educating but *training* volunteers. Surprisingly, many conservation groups do not have an official policy or procedure for training volunteers. Staff often simply make time to hastily outline what is to be done—often without explaining why the chore is important or what it hopes to accomplish. Alternatively, training consists of a stroll around the office with emphasis on the postage and copying machines. In these cases, you can basically say good-bye to many of your "trained" volunteers; they do not feel an integral part of your organization, so why waste their time?

Other programs or organizations, such as the Volunteers In Parks (VIP) program, the Student Conservation Association (SCA), the National Audubon Society, and the Izaak Walton League of America, train volunteers in the field. According to staff, of the twelve weeks a volunteer spends participating in the average SCA program, one to two weeks are spent in training. Participants in the VIP program within the National Park System are trained on site that day and throughout their stay by conservation professionals or agency staff. The national coordinator for the Izaak Walton League's Save Our Streams program travels throughout the United States giving one-day workshops that include slide shows on stream ecology, hands-on biological stream monitoring, and sign-up of attendees who want to adopt and monitor their own waterways.

Still known to those outside the conservation movement as the "bird-watchers' organization," the National Audubon Society has taken many years to develop a strong network of volunteers who work on numerous conservation issues unrelated to birding. To help make the transition from outdoor observer to outdoor activist, Audubon holds one-week volunteer leadership training seminars on lobbying, media strategy, and outdoor skills development in Washington, D.C. Upon completion of the seminar, participants are taken to Capitol Hill to put their lessons to work. Audubon also holds other, issue-oriented workshops at the state level to keep its members and the general public updated on various conservation issues. "The tradition of bird-watching has basically provided the foundation for Audubon's dynamic activist network," says Carlson.

Volunteer training should be considered in the same light as training of paid staff. Granted, even *that* training is often quick, sporadic, and given little or no follow-up, but a serious effort must be made to empower conservation volunteers by educating and inspiring them. An unskilled army is essentially an impotent army.

But how do we attract this army of volunteers in the first place? Who are they, and how can we find and reach them? We now come to the second fact regarding conservation volunteers: An "average" profile of these people does not exist. Gone is the stereotypical environmentalist with his beard, his sloppy clothes, and his tie-dyed, 1960s mentality. The conservation volunteer of the nineties is the five-year-old who is adopting her backyard stream, the corporate business professional looking to spend a few hours of physical activity in the outdoors, the senior citizen who fears for the future of his grandchildren.

If we want to change public policy in the next century, we've got to appeal to the public as a whole *and* as individuals. The Nature Conservancy, with its computerized data base of volunteers, is working to match its multiple needs with those of its volunteers. Sixty-eight-year-old Bob Byrne—volunteer coordinator at the Conservancy's national headquarters in Arlington, Virginia—is himself a volunteer. After contacting the American Association of Retired Persons' (AARP) volunteer network, he was told to give the conservancy a call. Now he works one day a week, monitoring upwards of twenty volunteers and attracting more people to help the Conservancy's national staff. He also fields calls from people across the country who are looking for local volunteer opportunities.

"The first thing people want to know is what kind of activities they'd be involved in," Byrne explains. "Then they want to know what times are available and what the organization does." He sends them a packet of general conservancy information and a volunteer application form, which is filled out and returned to the national or local office. The form asks for important background information, such as when the people are available, what their interests are, and what kinds of activities they want to do. Internally, each of the conservancy's field offices develops volunteer "job descriptions." The applicant is then matched as closely as possible with a "job," which may include everything from clerical work to data collection to physical labor on a wildlife preserve.

Volunteers, however, make the final choice, such as doing wildlife counts, transporting wild animals from one site to another, or eliminating exotic plants infringing on native plant populations. Like the work available, the backgrounds of conservancy volunteers are diverse. Many are retired, according to Byrne; others are homemakers with young children or students volunteering during summer and school breaks. Most have a good educational background, usually at the college level, and all have a deep interest in environmental and ecological issues. Volunteers are from sixteen to eighty years old—a range confirmed by numerous other conservation organizations and natural resource agencies. Women outnumber men slightly, but the difference is negligible.

While the stereotypical environmentalist evokes visions of men and women in their twenties and thirties, in the 1990s a growing number of volunteer senior citizens are playing an important role in conservation organizations. Mary Fuchs, who is eighty-one, has served as volunteer librarian-historian of the Izaak Walton League for fifteen years. Like Byrne, she had not participated in the environmental movement until she came to the organization. "I got hooked on conservation *after* I got there," she says. "After learning what was going on at the league and its history, I got interested. When you volunteer for a conservation organization, you are not just giving something to your community—you are making a contribution to the world. And it's something important, unlike stuffing envelopes for a mailing house or selling shoes."

Fuchs thinks seniors are especially beneficial to the conservation movement because the issues are so broad, thus requiring input from people who are experienced in a wide range of professional fields, including education, sociology, economics, labor, government, and administration. Seniors, meanwhile, find conservation organizations "a good way to apply old skills in a new area," Fuchs says. They also enjoy associating with younger people, anticipating daily volunteer activities, learning new skills, finding fresh interests and a sense of direction, and garnering respect from friends and family, who often worry about older relatives, she notes.

With no average profile set in stone, conservation organizations are at a disadvantage on how best to attract volunteers. Standard advertising is difficult to target when the potential audience is so large and diverse. While ads in local newspapers, publicity through organization publications, and public service announcements on radio and television help get the word out, an increasing number of organizations are turning to community volunteer clearinghouses, such as the AARP service that brought Bob Byrne into the fold. Listing volunteer opportunities is usually free or available for a nominal fee at these clearinghouses, and just about every state and county already offers these services. (Check the yellow pages in your local telephone book for a full listing.)

In response to student and public pressure, colleges and universities are also expanding or establishing similar distribution centers for volunteers. Several conservation volunteer coordinators say they do yearly mailings to major universities, which either post volunteer opportunities on bulletin boards or file them in internship or job-opportunity notebooks available for student perusal.

In some university courses, volunteering for nonprofit groups is actually required schoolwork. At Boston University, for instance, students enrolled in a course on the role of special-interest groups in public policy-making had to volunteer several hours a week to a group of their choice. A number turned to the Massachusetts Public Interest Research Group (MASSPIRG), which at the time was working on bottle-bill legislation, voter registration drives, and a public education campaign on recycling.

"Just about all my friends were working for either MASSPIRG or a PIRG in their own state," said one recent college graduate. "I hadn't really been into environmental issues before, but once I got involved, I became alarmed at where I saw our planet heading—down the tubes. Now, even though my course is over, I still volunteer for several different environmental groups. I've even had a chance to develop some skills that will help me with my career, like working as part of a team and learning professional office behavior."

The Student Conservation Association, headquartered in Charlestown, New Hampshire, is another volunteer clearinghouse that has brought thousands of young men and women into the conservation movement—both as professionals and as lifelong volunteers. Once accepted into the competitive Resource Assistant Program, started in 1957, volunteers fill the same niche as seasonal employees in conservation agencies. In 1990 the SCA expected to place 850 "natural resource assistants" throughout the states, the Virgin Islands, and Puerto Rico in agencies such as the National Park Service, the U.S. Fish and Wildlife Service, the Bureau of Land Management, and a few state agencies and private organizations.

Volunteer duties cover what the agencies do: giving interpretive programs, guiding hikes through backcountry, excavating archaeological sites, or serving as river rangers. At Glacier Bay National Park, for instance, SCA volunteers are studying humpback whales, while their counterparts at Voyageurs National Park are examining wolf populations.

"They [volunteers] basically are incorporated into the staff in the areas where they work," says Wallace Elton, program director for the Resource Assistant Program. Because two to three times as many people apply as can be accepted, the application process for the two core SCA programs is extensive and competitive. While the belief in environmental protection may be what initially attracts applicants to the SCA, so too is the opportunity to find employment in natural resource fields later. Conservation organizations must not ignore the fact that development of personal and professional skills is a primary motivation for volunteerism. And, with the competition for conservation jobs heating up, young workers and mid-life career changers are as eager to receive from their volunteer experience as they are to give of their time and talents.

Taking the time to talk to individuals about what they'd like to get out of volunteering is an important first step toward making them feel important to your organization. Helping volunteers reach personal goals garners strong loyalty, good morale, and improved dependability, agree volunteer coordinators.

Twenty-four-year-old Eunice Groark of Arlington, Virginia, worked two unpaid internships before landing her first paid conservation job at the Environmental Defense Fund. "I saw volunteering for a conservation group as an opportunity to educate myself on environmental issues, as well as just to learn about what other organizations existed and what the potential was to work as a staff member for them after I graduated," Groark explains. "I liked the feeling I was making a difference—that's very important to me—and I also enjoyed the atmosphere. I felt that people at both internships were enthusiastic and supportive. I'm still very close friends with some of my former co-workers."

While majoring in environmental policy at Syracuse University in New York, Groark worked for the New York PIRG, coordinating a countywide environmental group on recycling, pressuring university administrators to start a campus recycling program, talking to student groups about environmental protection, and organizing a pilot recycling day for college students. The university has since started a newspaper recycling program.

"I chose to volunteer for NYPIRG because they were making great strides in educating people on environmental and consumer issues on campus," she says. "I was impressed with them. Working with them, I really got the feeling I could do something and that I was handling a lot of important responsibilities."

That "I-can-have-an-impact" attitude is one of the first comments made by volunteers asked why they do what they do. The same is true of many paid staff members. Still, paid staff should be reminded regularly to keep their tones and words upbeat and supportive around volunteers, and even the smallest victory—for example, an editorial supportive of the organization's stand on an issue—should be celebrated at the next staff meeting.

To help keep volunteers, Groark suggests clarifying why the individual wants to give time to your organization: "If they're there just to fill up time, make sure they're busy. If a volunteer is interested specifically in a field, it's important to challenge them and to give them an opportunity to learn more about the field so they can move on to pursue a career or whatever else they're after. I'd also encourage them to attend meetings on environmental issues—both at the organization and in the community, like at a public hearing."

Groark's suggestions are good ones. In fact, few of the volunteers I spoke with had more than a second's pause when asked what could be done to better attract, keep, and utilize volunteers. Their lengthy list of ideas, discussed later, brings me to the third fact on which many of my fellow conservation professionals agree. It is simply this: We have failed. We, the conservation movement and its leaders, have failed to mobilize and inspire the mass support we must have to push through tough conservation legislation; we have failed to convince industries and governments to make environmental protection a top priority; and we have failed to spark the kind of citizen concern that inspires drastic social change.

Decades ago the voices, votes, and actions of an incensed American public managed to pull the nation out of war. Today, as we near the birth of a new century, we face a similar life-threatening crisis; the survival of our planet is at stake. Atmospheric warming, loss of fertile topsoil, groundwater contamination, tropical rain forest depletion, disappearing wildlife species—these are global environmental emergencies that require public input, a worldwide brainstorming for possible solutions to these daunting problems, and a foundation of millions—even hundreds of millions—of informed, determined, "hell-bent-for-election" conservation activists.

The number of such environmentalists in the United States is growing, according to just about every public poll within the past few years. Why, then, if more than three-fourths of the people consider themselves environmentalists and a large percentage rank environmental protection as the country's top concern, are our elected officials not jumping at our command? Why are world leaders not listening to our calls for global, as well as domestic, environmental strategies? No one likes to admit that we are still a clumsy movement, a movement largely unprepared to tackle the increasingly complex problems facing us.

As conservation professionals and grass-roots activists, we must find ways to tap into the virgin "green" territory that will make the difference to our future, our natural resources, and our generations to come. Promoting volunteerism and actively recruiting volunteers from all sectors of society can create, solidify, and build on the mass movement that is needed to change humanity's current course of self-destruction.

What are some practical steps that organizations can take to make better use of volunteers? The following list has been culled from numerous interviews with volunteers in various conservation organizations. While not every suggestion will work for every organization, all are at least worth some thought.

- *Take time to give volunteers an office tour and introduce them to staff.* Knowing what the layout of the office is, where supplies are, how to use the kitchen coffee maker—all are basic points of reference that are important to making volunteers feel welcome and integrated into the office team. *A volunteer information kit*—with the group's publications, historical background, membership brochure, annual report, staff and title list, telephone extension directory, and so forth—is also helpful.
- *Match tasks with skills and experience, and don't glamorize a job so much that volunteers are disappointed when they find themselves standing in front of the copying machine for two hours.* Start with simple chores—stuffing envelopes, organizing files—so they can get a taste of success and you can judge their ability to handle more difficult or crucial work. Don't expect everyone to do the same

amount of work; people's attention spans and levels of commitment vary. Don't give volunteers duties that are beyond their scope; they soon become discouraged and leave. As soon as possible, move volunteers into more meaningful work. Sure, they will do their share of stuffing envelopes, but it is not as hard to accept if they feel their volunteer job in general is personally challenging and assists the organization in its goals.

· *Don't let volunteers burn out.* It is easy to take a bright, enthusiastic volunteer and pile on a heavy load of "due-yesterday" projects. Resist the urge. Try not to always call on the same individuals when projects arise on short notice, and by all means don't make them feel guilty for giving less time than what would be most convenient for you or your organization. Alternate serious "brainwork" tasks with lighter responsibilities, and avoid giving urgent deadlines if possible.

· *Show them a good time.* I don't want to spend eight hours a day doing something dull, unchallenging, or frustrating; volunteers don't either—and they won't. Make sure they are introduced to everyone in the office and to each other so that a positive atmosphere of fellowship keeps volunteers coming back for more. Also be sure to include volunteers in office social events, such as birthday parties; this makes people feel like one of the staff and provides a chance to enjoy the group under more relaxed circumstances.

· *Draw volunteers into your mission.* Talk up the importance of teamwork in achieving your organization's goals, but recognize each volunteer as an individual. Treat volunteers with the professional and personal respect you give paid staff members. This means you must be clear about what you expect of them, such as dependability, and what you do not accept as office behavior, such as general gossip gatherings. From day one, volunteers should be gently discouraged from roaming the halls and tying up staff time with long-winded conversation.

· *Train new conservation leaders.* As I once heard a speaker on management say, "Have more chiefs than Indians." Look for those individuals with leadership potential and the skills you need, and train them early to be good leaders. Assign them to work with more experienced people who could serve as friends, supervisors, and mentors. Gradually give them more challenging work to do, always asking if they feel comfortable with one skill before moving them on to another. Boost self-confidence by providing them with opportunities to solve problems on their own.

· *Cover small expenses.* When asked, volunteers said they feel more valued and respected if they are reimbursed for their expenses. Driving expenses, for instance, can begin to add up, especially for students, senior citizens, and the unemployed. Most of your volunteers may not even ask to be reimbursed, but don't forfeit effective supporters because you can't find $20 to help cover their costs.

· *Consider providing transportation.* Many of the people with the most time, money, and life experience on hand—senior citizens—do not drive. Others simply may not own cars, live near public transportation, or have the physical capabilities required to be a driver.

This does not mean that they would not be more than happy to contribute their time to your cause. Talk to staff about providing a few free rides for such volunteers. Taking a few extra minutes during a staff person's morning commute should be more than compensated for by the extra amount of work accomplished.

· *Keep volunteers up to date on the progress of your effort.* Make sure volunteers are invited to participate in staff meetings so that everyone knows what new projects are under way and how the organization is doing in reaching its goals. You can always call a "department head" meeting at another time if you need to discuss issues more intimately.

Those organizations with a large army of volunteers might benefit from a newsletter designed specifically for volunteer needs and concerns. The newsletter could highlight current programs, interview field staff and volunteers, thank specific individuals, congratulate anyone and everyone for the slightest victory, and generally help keep volunteer morale high.

The publication does not have to be expensive or slick, just enthusiastic and informative. Type it on legal-size paper; glue on a few graphics for design; get it duplicated; and have a work party to fold, staple, address, and mail it. A publication geared to a select audience can create a strong tie among readers and provide a solid forum for discussion of volunteer issues.

As Eunice Groark says: "Be incredibly encouraging to volunteers [in your newsletters]. As a volunteer, you sometimes feel like you're the bottom rung on the stepladder, and it's important to believe that what you're doing is critical to the organization or to the cause."

Most of all, say thank you, thank you, thank you. Say it often. Say it loudly. Say it in public. Say it with flowers. I know of no conservation volunteer who gives time and energy in order to receive awards, nor do I know of a volunteer who has ever objected to receiving rewards.

Conservation Leadership Project Personnel

Staff

Patrick F. Noonan	President, The Conservation Fund
Donald Snow	Project Director and Editor
G. Jon Roush	Senior Associate
Laurie L. Hall	Project Assistant
Jean W. McKendry	Project Associate

Consultants

Joe W. Floyd	Eastern Montana College
Victoria Bomberry	Private Consultant
Dorceta E. Taylor	Yale University

Advisory Council

Lamar Alexander	University of Tennessee
Wallace Dayton	The Conservation Fund
Thomas Deans	New Hampshire Charitable Fund
George F. Dutrow	Duke University
George T. Frampton, Jr.	The Wilderness Society
Jerry F. Franklin	University of Washington
Ralph E. Grossi	American Farmland Trust

David F. Hales	Michigan Department of Natural Resources
Jean W. Hocker	Land Trust Alliance
Charles R. Jordan	City of Portland, Oregon, Bureau of Parks
Jack Lorenz	Izaak Walton League of America
Gerald P. McCarthy	Virginia Environmental Endowment
Lyle M. Nelson	Stanford University
Donal C. O'Brien	National Audubon Society
John C. Oliver III	Western Pennsylvania Conservancy
James Posewitz	Montana Department of Fish, Wildlife and Parks
Nathaniel P. Reed	1000 Friends of Florida
Henry R. Richmond	1000 Friends of Oregon
Daniel Simberloff	Florida State University
Hubert M. Vogelmann	University of Vermont
Norman K. Wessells	University of Oregon

Minorities Roundtable

David K. Baker	Private Consultant
Robert Bullard	University of California at Riverside
Cheryl A. Calloway	Michigan Department of Natural Resources
Marcia Chen	CEIP, Inc.
Clarice Gaylord	U.S. Environmental Protection Agency
Domingo Gonzales	Texas Center for Policy Studies
Kevin Gover	Gover, Williams, Stetson and West
Donna House	The Nature Conservancy
Collette Machado	Hui Alaloa
Anna Phillip	Inuit Circumpolar Conference
Gail Small	Native Action
Cris Stainbrook	Northwest Area Foundation

Robert Stanton   National Park Service
Gerry Stover   Environmental Consortium for
                                 Minority Outreach
Peterson Zah   Save the Children Federation

About the Editor

DONALD SNOW IS executive director of the Northern Lights Research & Education Institute and founder and editor of *Northern Lights Magazine* in Missoula, Montana. Since 1976 he has worked as a volunteer and staff member of several environmental organizations in the American West. He completed the Conservation Leadership Project as a staff associate to The Conservation Fund, based in Arlington, Virginia.

About the Contributors

JAMES E. CROWFOOT, professor of natural resources at the University of Michigan, served there as dean from 1983–1990. His research and teaching focuses on organizational management and change and conflict processes in relation to environmental and natural resource problems.

CHARLES R. JORDAN, superintendent of the Department of Parks and Recreation in Portland, Oregon, served on the President's Commission on Americans Outdoors and is a director of The Conservation Fund. A Gonzaga University graduate and a former Oxford University Fellow, Mr. Jordan chaired the Minority Roundtable of the Conservation Leadership Program and currently heads the advisory committee for the Conservation Career Development Program of the Student Conservation Association.

JACK LORENZ, executive director of the Izaak Walton League of America since 1974, has worked in industry and the nonprofit sector as a professional conservationist for more than twenty-five years. An ardent angler, Lorenz concentrates his stewardship efforts on protection of the nation's free-flowing streams and the establishment of a new outdoor ethic in America.

SALLY RANNEY is president and co-founder of American Wildlands. She is vice-president of the Island Foundation and serves as the co-ordinator of the POWER Project in Patagonia, Argentina. Ms. Ranney has been professionally involved in natural resource/environmental management for eighteen years. She was a resource policy analyst for The Wilderness Society and president of American Wilderness Adventures. She has served on the boards of several environmental organizations and was an appointed member of the President's Commission on Americans Outdoors.

NATHANIEL P. REED, president of 1000 Friends of Florida, is an active board member of the Natural Resources Defense Council and the National Geographic Society. Mr. Reed, a Florida businessman, was an Assistant Secretary of the Interior, served on the boards of the National Audubon Society and The Nature Conservancy, was chairman of the Florida Department of Air and Water Pollution Control, and headed the Governor's Commission on the Future of Florida's Environment.

ALDEMARO ROMERO is the founder and executive director of BIOMA, the Venezuelan Foundation for the Conservation of Biological Diversity. Dr. Romero is the author of over 250 scientific and popular articles on natural history and environmental sciences. He received his doctorate in tropical biology from the University of Miami, and his professorships include the University of Miami, as well as Venezuelan Central University and Metropolitan University, both in Caracas.

G. JON ROUSH, president of Canyon consulting, advises environmental groups and government agencies on strategic planning and management. His record of environmental leadership includes service as the executive vice-president and chairman of the board of The Nature Conservancy.

DANIEL SIMBERLOFF, Robert O. Lawton Distinguished Professor at Florida State University, has published many papers in ecology, evolution, biogeography, and conservation biology. He has chaired the science committees of The Nature Conservancy and Tall Timbers, Inc., and served on the editorial board of the Society for Conservation Biology. His conservation interests include refuge design, the effects of introduced species, and the organization of ecological communities.

JOANNA D. UNDERWOOD is founder and president of INFORM, Inc., the national nonprofit environmental research organization. Since its establishment in 1974, INFORM has been a prime force in educating decision-makers in business, government, the community, and the media about the need for a new preventive approach to environmental problems.

Index

Also Available from
Island Press

Natural Resources for the 21st Century
Edited by R. Neil Sampson and Dwight Hair

The New York Environment Book
By Eric A. Goldstein and Mark A. Izeman

Overtapped Oasis: Reform or Revolution for Western Water
By Marc Reisner and Sarah Bates

Permaculture: A Practical Guide for a Sustainable Future
By Bill Mollison

Plastics: America's Packaging Dilemma
By Nancy Wolf and Ellen Feldman

The Poisoned Well: New Strategies for Groundwater Protection
Edited by Eric Jorgensen

Race to Save the Tropics: Ecology and Economics for a Sustainable Future
Edited by Robert Goodland

Recycling and Incineration: Evaluating the Choices
By Richard A. Denison and John Ruston

Reforming the Forest Service
By Randal O'Toole

The Rising Tide: Global Warming and World Sea Levels
By Lynne T. Edgerton

Saving the Tropical Forests
By Judith Gradwohl and Russell Greenberg

Trees, Why Do You Wait?
By Richard Critchfield

War on Waste: Can America Win Its Battle with Garbage?
By Louis Blumberg and Robert Gottlieb

Western Water Made Simple
From *High Country News*

Wetland Creation and Restoration: The Status of the Science
Edited by Mary E. Kentula and Jon A. Kusler

Wildlife and Habitats in Managed Landscapes
Edited by Jon E. Rodiek and Eric G. Bolen

For a complete catalog of Island Press publications, please write
Island Press, Box 7, Covelo, CA 95428, or call 1-800-828-1302.